AEROFILMS GUIDE

FOOTBALL GROUNDS

EIGHTH REVISED EDITION

AEROFILMS GUIDE

FOOTBALL GROUNDS

EIGHTH REVISED EDITION

DIAL
HOUSE

CONTENTS

Front cover: The scale of Old Trafford — the self-styled 'Theatre of Dreams' — gets ever more impressive. With construction work continuing apace, the 1999/2000 season saw the ground stage the first Premier League games with crowds in excess of 60,000.

Back cover: Equally impressive, in its own way, is the transformation of Gresty Road by First Division Crewe Alexandra. For many the continuing survival of a team like Crewe under Dario Gradi is proof that it is possible for well-managed small-town clubs to prosper.

Preceding pages: The creation of 'Fortress St James' in Newcastle continues; dominating the local landscape, the rebuilt ground will ultimately have a capacity in excess of 50,000. At the other end of the spectrum, the Nationwide League welcomes Kidderminster Harriers' Aggborough Stadium for the start of the 2000/01 campaign.

First published in 1993;
Reprinted 1993 (twice); Second edition 1994; Third edition 1995; Fourth edition 1996; Fifth edition 1997; Sixth edition 1998; Seventh edition 1999; Eighth edition 2000.

ISBN 0 7110 2761 7

Published by Dial Hose
an imprint of Ian Allan Publishing Ltd, Terminal House, Shepperton, Surrey TW17 8AS; and printed by Ian Allan Printing Ltd, Riverdene Business Park, Hersham, Surrey KT12 4RG.

Code: 00/08

Text © Ian Allan Publishing Ltd 1993-2000
Diagrams © Ian Allan Publishing Ltd 2000
Aerial Photography © Aerofilms

Aerofilms Limited have been specialists in aerial photography since 1919. Their library of aerial photographs, both new and old, is in excess of 1.5 million images. Aerofilms undertake to commission oblique and vertical survey aerial photography, which is processed and printed in their specialised photographic laboratory. Digital photomaps are prepared using precision scanners.

Free photostatic proofs are available on request for any site held within the collection and price lists will be forwarded detailing the size of photographic enlargement available without any obligation to purchase.

Introduction

Welcome to the eighth edition of this guide to football grounds. As always, we have endeavoured to record all the changes to have affected grounds in the FA Carling Premier League and Nationwide Leagues. Inevitably, the pace of construction means that much of what is recorded here will be completed by the time that the season starts; none the less, as an indication of work in progress, the book records a remarkable level of investment in the national sport.

It is frightening to think that it is now 15 years since the fire at Valley Parade and more than a decade since the tragedy at Hillsborough. In the years since these two domestic tragedies, football has been through a revolution in both financial — courtesy of the money being ploughed into the television rights — and facility terms. There is now little or no comparison between the standards of football grounds today and those of 20 years ago. Moreover, as is evident from the number of grounds for which updated photography was required for this edition, football grounds continue to evolve at a frightening rate.

For the first time in a couple of years, there are no new grounds amongst existing members of the Nationwide League and Carling Premier League to record. Whilst a number of new grounds are planned — at Southampton and Swansea, for example — none have been completed for the new season. The one new entry is, therefore, Kidderminster Harriers. Few will begrudge the entry of the League's newest member as, some years ago, Harriers were cruelly denied promotion when their ground was deemed not to be up to League standards. Inevitably, one team's promotion means another's disappearance and in 1999/2000 the casualty was Chester City — the first team with a wholly new stadium to suffer this fate.

Another casualty is the old Wembley Stadium; the whole site, with its familiar twin towers will be demolished and replaced by a new national stadium as part of the ill-fated campaign to bring the 2006 World Cup to England. Whilst many will mourn the passing of the twin towers, Wembley's facilities were increasingly poor in comparison with those available elsewhere and the new stadium should prove to be immeasurably better than the old. Time will, however, tell as to whether it can generate the same atmosphere and history.

As always, at the start of the new season, fans everywhere will have high hopes for their team's success during the course of the season. Some will inevitably be disappointed, others will enjoy unexpected success. Whatever the fortunes of your team, enjoy the new season!

Disabled Facilities

We endeavour to list the facilities for disabled spectators at each ground. Readers will appreciate that these facilities can vary in number and quality and that, for most clubs, pre-booking is essential. Some clubs also have dedicated parking for disabled spectators; this again should be pre-booked if available.

WEMBLEY

Wembley Stadium, Wembley HA9 0DW

Tel No: 020 8795 5733
Advance Tickets Tel No: 020 8902 0902
Fax: 020 8900 1045
Brief History: Inaugurated for F.A. Cup Final of 1923, venue for many major national and international matches including World Cup Final in 1966. Also used for major occasion in other sports and as venues for rock concerts and other entertainments.
(Total) Current Capacity: 80,000 (all seated)
Nearest Railway Station: Wembley Stadium (BR), Wembley Central (BR & Tube), Wembley Park (tube)
Parking (Car): Limited parking at ground and nearby

Parking (Coach/Bus): As advised by police
Police Force: Metropolitan
Anticipated Development(s): After some wrangling, particularly over linked improvements to transport facilities in the area, Brent Council approved the redevelopment scheme for the stadium in early June. The £475 million scheme will see the construction of a 90,000-seat stadium, alongside a 200-bed hotel, office accommodation and visitor centre. It is planned that work will start immediately after the England-Germany World Cup qualifier, due to be held in October.

Above: 619600; Right: 619568

ARSENAL

Arsenal Stadium, Avenell Road, Highbury, London, N5 1BU

Tel No: 020 7704 4000
Advance Tickets Tel No: 020 7704 4040
Fax: 020 7704 4001
Web Site: www.arsenal.co.uk
League: F.A. Premier
Brief History: Founded 1886 as Royal Arsenal, changed to Woolwich Arsenal in 1891, and Arsenal in 1914. Former grounds: Plumstead Common, Sportsman Ground, Manor Ground (twice), moved to Arsenal Stadium (Highbury) in 1913. Record attendance 73,295
(Total) Current Capacity: 38,900 (all seated)
Visiting Supporters' Allocation: 2,900 (all seated Clock End and Lower Tier West Stand)
Club Colours: Red shirts with white sleeves, white shorts
Nearest Railway Station: Drayton Park or Finsbury Park (main line). Arsenal (tube)
Parking (Car): Street Parking
Parking (Coach/Bus): Drayton Park
Police Force and Tel No: Metropolitan (020 7263 9090)
Disabled Visitors' Facilities:
Wheelchairs: Lower tier East Stand
Blind: Commentary available
Anticipated Development(s): After some years of uncertainty as to the club's future strategy, given the fact that Highbury is small by the scale of leading Premier League teams and is unlikely to be extended, the club announced during the 1999/00 season that it was progressing with plans for a 60,000 all-seater stadium on a 25 acre site in Ashpurton Grove, about half-a-mile from Highbury.

KEY

C Club Offices
E Entrance(s) for visiting supporters

↑ North direction (approx)

❶ Avenell Road
❷ Highbury Hill
❸ Gillespie Road
❹ To Drayton Park BR Station (¼ mile)
❺ Arsenal Tube Station
❻ Clock End
❼ St Thomas's Road (to Finsbury Park station)

Finishing in second place — a considerable distance behind Manchester United, however — and reaching the final of the UEFA Cup, might imply that the Gunners had had a successful season. Looking more closely, however, at Arsene Wenger's team during the season, however, and all is not quite so rosy. The team qualified for the UEFA Cup through failure to progress in the Champions League — the choice of Wembley for the home games proving to be, arguably, a mistake — and the lacklustre performance in the final against Galatasary in Copenhagen meant that the team failed to add to the Highbury trophy cabinet. Domestically, the team also, on occasions, failed to perform well. Part of this failure must be down to the poor performances on a number of occasions by the club's star players. However, another place in the Champions League gives the team another opportunity to try and emulate Chelsea's relative success in the competition in 1999/2000.

ASTON VILLA

Villa Park, Trinity Road, Birmingham, B6 6HE

Tel No: 0121 327 2299
Advance Tickets Tel No: 0121 327 5353
Fax: 0121 322 2107
Web Site: www.avfc.co.uk
E-Mail: postmaster@astonvilla-fc.co.uk
League: F.A. Premier
Brief History: Founded in 1874. Founder Members Football League (1888). Former Grounds: Aston Park and Lower Aston Grounds and Perry Bar, moved to Villa Park (a development of the Lower Aston Grounds) in 1897. Record attendance 76,588
(Total) Current Capacity: 39,217 (all seated) (Prior to redevelopment)
Visiting Supporters' Allocation: Approx 2,983 in North Stand
Club Colours: Claret with blue stripe shirts, claret shorts

Nearest Railway Station: Witton
Parking (Car): Asda car park, Aston Hall Road
Parking (Coach/Bus): Asda car park, Aston Hall Road (special coach park for visiting supporters situated in Witton Lane)
Police Force and Tel No: West Midlands (0121 322 6010)
Disabled Visitors' Facilities:
  Wheelchairs: Trinity Road Stand section
  Blind: Commentary by arrangement
Anticipated Development(s): Work on the Trinity Road Stand commenced at the end of the 2000/01 season — unfortunately after the date the photographs were taken — with the demolition of the familiar and historic façade. This work and the reconstruction of the North Stand will lift Villa Park's capacity to 51,000 when completed.

KEY

C Club Offices
S Club Shop
E Entrance(s) for visiting supporters
R Refreshment bars for visiting supporters
T Toilets for visiting supporters

↑ North direction (approx)

❶ B4137 Witton Lane
❷ B4140 Witton Road
❸ Trinity Road
❹ A4040 Aston Lane to A34 Walsall Road
❺ To Aston Expressway & M6
❻ Holte End
❼ Visitors' Car Park
❽ Witton railway station
❾ North Stand
❿ Trinity Road Stand

Above: 684909; *Right:* 684899

A football club's season can often be determined by a single moment or game during the course of the season and, in Villa's case, it was the victory over Darlington in the FA Cup. Up until that point, the team had under-performed and the media vultures were starting to circle over John Gregory. If Villa hadn't won that game then, possibly, Gregory would not have seen out the season. In the event, Villa went on to finish sixth in the Premier League and reach the FA Cup final for the first time in 43 years. Unfortunately, a lacklustre performance in the final meant a 1-0 defeat and the prospect of attempting to qualify for Europe through the Intertoto Cup. With his talented squad, with youth combing well with experience, Gregory's team should again feature in the chase for silverware in 2000/01.

BARNET

Underhill Stadium, Barnet Lane, Barnet, Hert, EN2 2BE]

Tel No: 020 8441 6932
Advance Tickets Tel No: 020 849 6325
Fax: 020 8447 0655
League: 3rd Division
Brief History: Founded 1888 as Barnet Alston. Changed name to Barnet (1919). Former grounds: Queens Road and Totteridge Lane. Promoted to Football League 1991. Record attendance 11,026
(Total) Current Capacity: 5,500 (approx 1,000 seated)
Visiting Supporters' Allocation: 1,200 in South Stand
Club Colours: Amber shirts, amber shorts
Nearest Railway Station: New Barnet (High Barnet – Tube)
Parking (Car): Street Parking and High Barnet Station
Parking (Coach/Bus): As directed by Police

Police Force and Tel No: Metropolitan (020 8200 2212)
Disabled Visitors' Facilities:
Wheelchairs: Barnet Lane (Social Club end – few spaces)
Blind: No special facility
Anticipated Development(s): The club has again received a dispensation to retain Underhill for another season despite its low capacity and the club is currently undertaking work to ensure a 5,500 capacity (including 1,000 seats) by the League's 1 August deadline. A planning application has been made for a £12.7 million stadium to be built at Claremont Road in Cricklewood — home of Hendon — with the intention that this will be available for the start of the 2002/03 season.

KEY

C Club Offices
S Club Shop
E Entrance(s) for visiting supporters
R Refreshment bars for visiting supporters
T Toilets for visiting supporters

↑ North direction (approx)

❶ Barnet Lane
❷ Westcombe Drive
❸ A1000 Barnet Hill
❹ New Barnet BR station (1 mile)
❺ To High Barnet Tube Station, M1 & M25
❻ Social Club

BARNET LANE

| FAMILY STAND | MAIN STAND | N/WEST TERRACE UNCOVERED |

DISABLED ENCLOSURE

PITCH SIZE
115 X 75 yards

SOUTH STAND UNCOVERED AWAY SEATS

DISABLED FANS

NORTH TERRACE UNCOVERED

WESTCOMBE DRIVE

AWAY

3/4's COVERED
EAST TERRACE

PRIORY GROVE / FAIRFIELD WAY

Nemesis for Barnet in a season of some progress came in the form of former boss Barry Fry, whose current team Peterborough United knocked the Bees out of the Third Division play-offs at the semi-final stage. However, sixth place for John Still's team represented a considerable advance upon the 16th achieved in 1998/99. However, further progress will depend on resolving the on-going issue of the ground and, possibly, in keeping the manager, who was being linked with the vacant job at Conference side Stevenage at the end of the season.

BARNSLEY

Oakwell Ground, Grove Street, Barnsley, S71 1ET

Tel No: 01226 211211
Advance Tickets Tel No: 01226 211211
Fax: 01226 211444
Web Site: www.barnsleyfc.co.uk
E-mail: thereds@barnsleyfc.co.uk
League: 1st Division
Brief History: Founded in 1887 as Barnsley St Peter's, changed name to Barnsley in 1897. Former Ground: Doncaster Road, Worsboro Bridge until 1888. Record attendance 40,255
(Total) Current Capacity: 23,009 (all seated)
Visiting Supporters' Allocation: 6,000 maximum (all seated; North Stand)
Club Colours: Red shirts, white shorts
Nearest Railway Station: Barnsley Exchange
Parking (Car): Queen's Ground car park

Parking (Coach/Bus): Queen's Ground car park
Police Force and Tel No: South Yorkshire (01266 206161)
Disabled Visitors' Facilities:
Wheelchairs: Purpose Built Disabled Stand
Blind: Commentary available
Future Development(s): With the completion of the new North Stand with its 6,000 capacity, the next phase for the redevelopment of Oakwell will feature the old West Stand with its remaining open seating. There is, however, no timescale for this work

KEY

C Club Offices
S Club Shop
E Entrance(s) for visiting supporters

⬆ North direction (approx)

❶ A628 Pontefract Road
❷ To Barnsley Exchange BR station and M1 Junction 37 (two miles)
❸ Queen's Ground Car Park
❹ North Stand
❺ Grove Street
❻ To Town Centre

Above: 685529; Right: 685527

Under the experienced Dave Bassett, Barnsley discovered the form that took them up to the Premier League and made a determined push towards the automatic promotion spots. Unfortunately, the team was unable to hold on to one of these and had to be satisfied with a creditable fourth place. Defeat of Birmingham City in the Play-Offs — assisted by a thumping 4-0 win at St Andrews — took the Tykes to Wembley for the first time in the club's history (when the team won the FA Cup before World War 1 the final was played at Crystal Palace). One of the relatively few teams never to have graced the twin towers, Barnsley took on Play-Off regulars Ipswich Town on Monday 29 May. Unfortunately, despite Barnsley going 1-0 up and having a penalty saved just before half time, Ipswich were to come out victorious 4-2 leaving Bassett's team to face another scramble in 2000/01 to regain its Premier League spot.

BIRMINGHAM CITY

St Andrew's, St Andrew's Street, Birmingham, B9 4NH

Tel No: 0121 772 0101
Advance Tickets Tel No: 0121 772 0101
Fax: 0121 766 7866
Web Site: www.bcfc.com
League: 1st Division
Brief History: Founded 1875, as Small Heath Alliance. Changed to Small Heath in 1888, Birmingham in 1905, Birmingham City in 1945. Former Grounds: Arthur Street, Ladypool Road, Muntz Street, moved to St Andrew's in 1906. Record attendance 68,844
(Total) Current Capacity: 30,018 (all seated)
Visiting Supporters' Allocation: 1-4,500 in new Railway End (Lower Tier)
Club Colours: Blue shirts, white shorts
Nearest Railway Station: Birmingham New Street

Parking (Car): Street parking
Parking (Coach/Bus): Coventry Road
Police Force and Tel No: West Midlands (0121 772 1169)
Disabled Visitors' Facilities:
  Wheelchairs: 90 places; advanced notice required
  Blind: Commentary available
Future Development(s): With the completion of the rebuilding of the Railway End, attention has turned to the old Main Stand. There are proposals for the construction of a 7,500-seat stand, which would also incorporate a hotel and conference centre. There is no definite time scale for this project, which would conclude the rebuilding of St Andrews.

KEY

C Club Offices
S Club Shop
E Entrance(s) for visiting supporters

↑ North direction (approx)

❶ Car Park
❷ B4128 Cattell Road
❸ Tilton Road
❹ Garrison Lane
❺ To A4540 & A38 (M)
❻ To City Centre and New Street BR Station (1½ miles)
❼ Railway End
❽ Tilton Road End
❾ Main Stand
❿ Kop Stand
⓫ Emmeline Street
⓬ Kingston Road
⓭ St Andrew's Street

Above: 679483; Right: 679479

A season of moderate success, despite the team's injury problems, saw City reach the Play-Offs as widely predicted. However, defeat by Barnsley over the two legs — including an embarrassing 4-0 reverse at St Andrews — has condemned Trevor Francis's team to another season of First Division football. With local rivals Aston Villa having considerable success in the Premier League and reaching the FA Cup final to boot, City's long-suffering fans will start to get restless if the team fails to make a determined stride towards automatic promotion in 2000/01. Another season of missed opportunities could see Francis the victim of the David Sullivan's ambitions for the club.

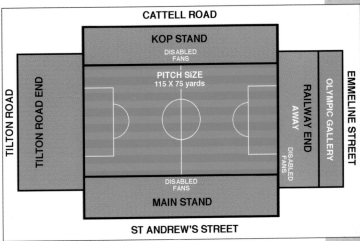

CATTELL ROAD

KOP STAND

DISABLED FANS

PITCH SIZE
115 X 75 yards

TILTON ROAD

TILTON ROAD END

RAILWAY END AWAY

DISABLED FANS

OLYMPIC GALLERY

EMMELINE STREET

DISABLED FANS

MAIN STAND

ST ANDREW'S STREET

BLACKBURN ROVERS

Ewood Park, Blackburn, Lancashire, BB2 4JF

Tel No: 01254 698888
Advance Tickets Tel No: 01254 671666
Fax: 01254 671042
Web Site: www.rovers.co.uk
E-Mail: enquiries@rovers.co.uk
League: 1st Division
Brief History: Founded 1875. Former Grounds:
  Oozebooth, Pleasington Cricket Ground,
  Alexandra Meadows. Moved to Ewood Park in
  1890. Founder members of Football League
  (1888). Record attendance 61,783
(Total) Current Capacity: 31,367 (all seated)
Visiting Supporters' Allocation: 3,914 at the
  Darwen End

Club Colours: Blue and white halved shirts,
  white shorts
Nearest Railway Station: Blackburn
Parking (Car): Street parking
Parking (Coach/Bus): As directed by Police
Police Force and Tel No: Lancashire (01254
  51212)
Disabled Visitors' Facilities:
  Wheelchairs: All sides of the ground
  Blind: Commentary available
Anticipated Development(s): There is talk
  that the Walkersteel Stand may be rebuilt, but
  this is very tentative at this stage.

KEY

C Club Offices
S Club Shop
E Entrance(s) for visiting supporters
R Refreshment bars for visiting supporters
T Toilets for visiting supporters

⬆ North direction (approx)

❶ A666 Bolton Road
❷ Kidder Street
❸ Nuttall Street
❹ Town Centre & Blackburn Central BR station (1½ miles)
❺ To Darwen and Bolton
❻ Car parking area for 500 cars
❼ Car Parks
❽ Top O'Croft Road

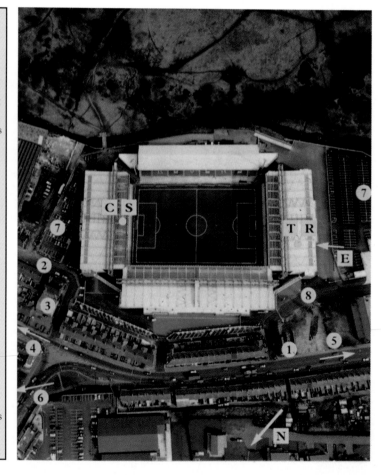

One of the pre-season favourites for an immediate return to the Premier League, the Brian Kidd-managed Blackburn Rovers started the season with deplorable form and, for much of the first half of the season, appeared relegation rather than promotion candidates. For an ambitious team like Blackburn, this was unacceptable and Kidd paid for the team's lack of success with his job with former Liverpool manager Graeme Souness taking over the reins ultimately. Although the second half of the season was more productive, the Jack Walker-financed team was never able to make a sustained challenge for even a Play-Off spot and a further season in the First Division beckons. With the Premier League financial 'umbrella' running out at the end of 2000/01, Rovers' future might be considered bleak if a return to the top flight isn't engineered this season particularly given Jack Walker's recent death.

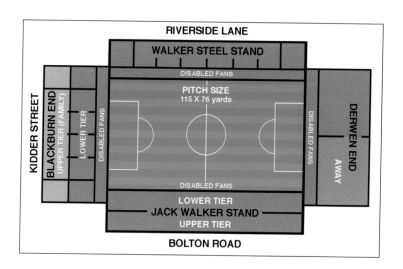

BLACKPOOL

Bloomfield Road, Blackpool, Lancashire, FY1 6JJ

Tel No: 01253 405331
Advance Tickets Tel No: 01253 444331
Fax: 01253 405011
E-Mail: bfc@cyberspace.net
League: 3rd Division
Brief History: Founded 1887, merged with 'South Shore' (1899). Former grounds: Raikes Hall (twice) and Athletic Grounds, Stanley Park, South Shore played at Cow Cap Lane, moved to Bloomfield Road in 1899. Record attendance 38,098
(Total) Current Capacity: 6,312 (1,521 seated)
Visiting Supporters' Allocation: 1,040
Club Colours: Tangerine shirts, tangerine shorts
Nearest Railway Station: Blackpool South
Parking (Car): At Ground and street parking (also behind West Stand – from M55)
Parking (Coach/Bus): Mecca car park (behind North End (also behind West Stand – from M55)
Police Force and Tel No: Lancashire (01253 293933)
Disabled Visitors' Facilities:
  Wheelchairs: By players entrance
  Blind: Commentary available (limited numbers)
Anticipated Development(s): After some years of uncertainty, work started in the close season on the redevelopment of Bloomfield Road with the demolition of the Kop and West Stand during the close season. This will temporarily reduce the ground's capacity to the figures mentioned above. It is hoped that the new facilities will be open during the course of the new season.

KEY

C Club Offices
S Club Shop
E Entrance(s) for visiting supporters
R Refreshment bars for visiting supporters
T Toilets for visiting supporters

↑ North direction (approx)

❶ Car Park
❷ To Blackpool South BR Station (1½ miles) and M55 Junction 4
❸ Bloomfield Drive
❹ Central Drive
❺ Henry Street
❻ Blackpool Greyhound Stadium
❼ Blackpool Tower

Above: 613777

Whilst the Second Division saw a couple of teams with an historic pedigree filling the automatic promotion spots, Blackpool was, unfortunately, not one of them. Under Nigel Worthington the team was much more interested in events at the wrong end of the table. Relegation to the Third Division is made all the more bitter for fans of the Seasiders by the fact that local rivals Preston North End won the Second Division championship and will, therefore, be facing teams of the calibre of Sheffield Wednesday and Nottingham Forest rather than those to be found in the Nationwide League's basement division. In a year which saw the death of one of Blackpool's greatest stars — Stanley Matthews — the fact that a team that once graced the old First Division and won the FA Cup is now languishing in the Nationwide League's lowest division shows how far the game has changed over the past few decades.

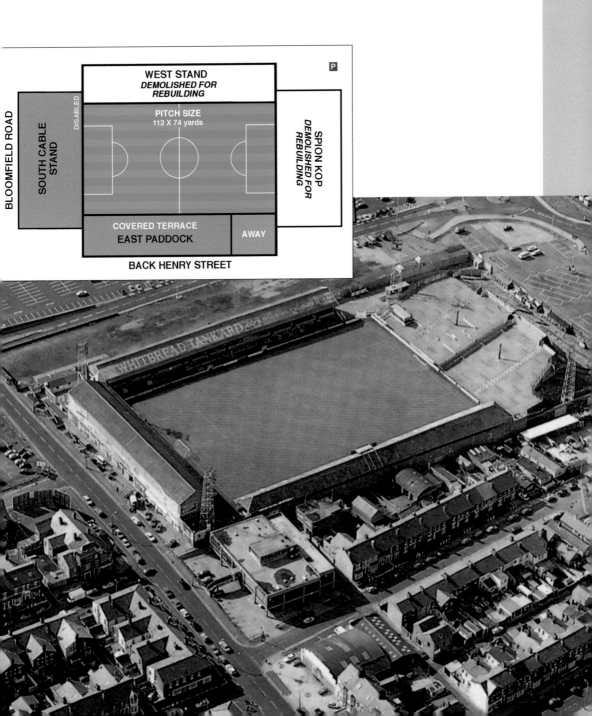

BOLTON WANDERERS

Reebok Stadium, Burnden Way, Lostock, Bolton, BL6 6JW

Tel No: 01204 673673
Advance Tickets Tel No: 01204 673601
Fax: 01204 673773
E-Mail: admin@bwfc.co.uk
Web Site: www.boltonfc.co.uk
League: 1st Division
Brief History: Founded 1874 as Christ Church;
name changed 1877. Former grounds: Several
Fields, Pikes Lane (1880-95) and Burnden
Park (1895-1997). Moved to Reebok Stadium
for 1997/98 season. Record attendance
(Burnden Park): 69,912. Record attendance of
25,000 at Reebok Stadium first achieved on 20
September 1997
(Total) Current Capacity: 27,800 (all-seater)
Visiting Supporters' Allocation: 5,200 (South
Stand)

Club Colours: White shirts, blue shorts
Nearest Railway Station: Horwich Parkway
Parking (Car): 2,000 places at ground with up
to 3,000 others in proximity
Parking (Coach/Bus): As directed
Police Force and Tel No: Greater Manchester
(01204 522466)
Disabled Visitors' Facilities:
Wheelchairs: c150 places around the ground
Blind: Commentary available
Anticipated Developments(s): The station at
Horwich Parkway has now opened. There are
currently no further plans for the development
of the Reebok Stadium.

KEY
↑ North direction (approx)
❶ Junction 6 of M61
❷ A6027 Horwich link road
❸ South Stand (away)
❹ North Stand
❺ Nat Lofthouse Stand
❻ West Stand
❼ M61 northbound to M6 and Preston
❽ M61 southbound to Manchester
❾ To Horwich and Bolton
❿ To Lostock Junction BR station
⓫ Horwich Parkway station

Above: 679726; Right: 679725

Widely expected to feature in the First Division Play-Offs at the start of the season, Colin Todd's team did not disappoint, although it required a change of manager — with Sam Allardyce taking over — and a strong run towards the end of the season, combined with Huddersfield Town's loss of form to ensure that the team grabbed sixth place. Given that this meant that Wanderers would face Ipswich Town in the semi-final, many would no doubt have fancied Wanderers to make a final return to Wembley given the East Anglian team's reputation for failure at this stage in the previous three seasons. A Wembley visit, in the ground's final full season, would have had a nice symmetry, given that Bolton were one of the teams that competed for the first FA Cup there. However, Ipswich clearly had no sense of history as, after extra time at Portman Road, it was Town that battled through 8-5 on aggregate. It was a close run affair, though, as the East Anglians equalised in the last few minutes of normal time to force extra time in the first place.

A.F.C. BOURNEMOUTH

Dean Court, Bournemouth, Dorset, BH7 7AF

Tel No: 01202 395381
Advance Tickets Tel No: 01202 395381
Fax: 01202 309797
E-Mail: enquiries@afcb.co.uk
Web Site: www.afcb.co.uk
League: 2nd Division
Brief History: Founded 1890 as Boscombe St. John's, changed to Boscombe (1899), Bournemouth & Boscombe Athletic (1923) and A.F.C. Bournemouth (1971). Former grounds Kings Park (twice) and Castlemain Road, Pokesdown. Moved to Dean Court in 1910. Record attendance 28,799
(Total) Current Capacity: 10,770 (3,141 seated)
Visiting Supporters' Allocation: 2,770 (150 seated A Block Stand only)
Club Colours: Red and black shirts, black shorts

Nearest Railway Station: Bournemouth
Parking (Car): Large car park adjacent ground
Parking (Coach/Bus): Large car park adjacent ground
Police Force and Tel No: Dorset (01202 552099)
Disabled Visitors' Facilities:
Wheelchairs: South Stand (prior arrangement)
Blind: No special facility
Anticipated Development(s): Having abandoned the possibility of rebuilding Dean Court, the club announced plans for the construction of a new stadium on the A338 Wessex Way. It is hoped that work will start on the new stadium in early 2001 with the intention that it will open for the 2001/02 season. However, at the time of writing, these plans are by no means certain to progress.

KEY

C Club Offices
S Club Shop
E Entrance(s) for visiting supporters
R Refreshment bars for visiting supporters
T Toilets for visiting supporters

↑ North direction (approx)

❶ Car Park
❷ A338 Wessex Way
❸ To Bournemouth BR Station (1½ miles)
❹ To A31 & M27
❺ Thistlebarrow Road
❻ King's Park Drive
❼ Littledown Avenue
❽ A3049 Ashley Road

Having missed out on the Play-Offs at the end of the 1998/99 season, many considered that Mel Machin's Bournemouth would reach them in 1999/2000. In the event, the team went in reverse during the course of the season and ultimately finished a disappointing 16th. As such the Cherries were never in danger of dropping into the relegation battle, but equally, being more than 20 points off the Play-Off zone at the end, never really featured in the promotion race. With an end of season clear out seeing the departure of a number of familiar faces, including Mark Stein (whose goals had been a consistent aid to the team's performances in recent years), it looks as though 2000/01 will be another torrid season for fans.

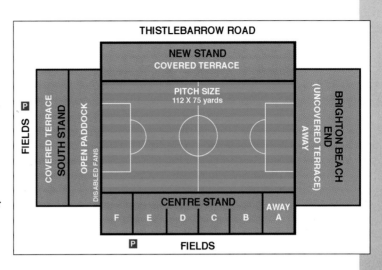

BRADFORD CITY

Bradford & Bingley Stadium, Valley Parade, Bradford, BD8 7DY

Tel No: 01274 773355
Advance Tickets Tel No: 01274 770022
Fax: 01274 773356
Web Site: www.bradfordcityfc.co.uk
E-Mail: bradfordcityfc@compuserve.com
League: F.A. Premier
Brief History: Founded 1903 (formerly Manningham Northern Union Rugby Club founded in 1876). Continued use of Valley Parade, joined 2nd Division on re-formation. Record attendance: 39,146
(Total) Current Capacity: 18,276 (all seated)
Visiting Supporters' Allocation: 1,842 (all seated) in Symphony stand
Club Colours: Claret and amber shirts, claret shorts
Nearest Railway Station: Bradford Forster Square

Parking (Car): Street parking and car parks
Parking (Coach/Bus): As directed by Police
Police Force and Tel No: West Yorkshire (01274 723422)
Disabled Visitors' Facilities:
   Wheelchairs: 110 places in Sunwin, CIBA and Carlsberg stands
   Blind: Commentary available
Anticipated Development(s): Following completion of the Carlsberg Stand for the start of the 1999/2000 season, work started towards the end of the season on the construction the expansion of the Sunwin Stand and on the corner in-fill between the Carlsberg and Sunwin stands. It is hoped that this work will be completed during the course of the 2000/01 season and take the capacity of Valley Parade up to about 25,000.

KEY
- **C** Club Offices
- **S** Club Shop
- **E** Entrance(s) for visiting supporters
- **R** Refreshment bars for visiting supporters
- **T** Toilets for visiting supporters

⬆ North direction (approx)

❶ Midland Road
❷ Valley Parade
❸ A650 Manningham Lane
❹ To City Centre, Forster Square and Interchange BR Stations M606 & M62
❺ To Keighley
❻ Car Parks
❼ Sunwin Stand (being rebuilt)
❽ Midland (CIBA) Stand
❾ Symphony Stand
❿ Carlsberg Stand

Above: 685541; Right: 685534

THORNCLIFFE ROAD

CARLSBERG STAND

UPPER — M L K J H G
LOWER — F E D C B A

MIDLAND ROAD

CIBA STAND

A	B	C	D	E	F	G
DISABLED FANS						

PITCH SIZE
113 X 75

DISABLED FANS

F	E	D	C	B	A

SUNWIN STAND

SOUTH PARADE

SYMPHONY STAND

AWAY LOWER — UPPER

HOLYWELL ASH LANE

The dream lives on! Despite being most pundits' automatic favourites for an automatic return to the First Division, the Bantams survived the drama of the last day — where they defeated Liverpool and Southampton defeated Wimbledon — to face a second season in the Premier League. Although the team gathered the lowest number of points by any survivor since 1982, the players' spirit helped them to a number of notable successes during the course of the season. Victories over Arsenal and Liverpool at home and at Sunderland and Middlesbrough away were amongst the high points. No doubt most pundits will again see City as favourites for the drop in 2000/01, but many fans — and not only those from Bradford — will secretly be hoping that the team can once again defy the odds and keep romance alive in the Premier League. Bring on Rodney Marsh .....

BRENTFORD

Griffin Park, Braemar Road, Brentford, Middlesex, TW8 0NT

Tel No: 020 8847 2511
Advance Tickets Tel No: 020 8847 2511
Fax: 020 8568 9940
Web Site: www.brentford.fc.co.uk
E-Mail: enquiries@brentfordfc.co.uk
League: 2nd Division
Brief History: Founded 1889. Former Grounds: Clifden House Ground, Benn's Field (Little Ealing), Shotters Field, Cross Roads, Boston Park Cricket Ground, moved to Griffin Park in 1904. Founder-members Third Division (1920). Record attendance 38,678
(Total) Current Capacity: 12,750 (8,907 seated)
Visiting Supporters' Allocation: 2,263 (636 seated) in Brook Street Stand
Club Colours: Red and white striped shirts, black shorts

Nearest Railway Station: Brentford, South Ealing (tube)
Parking (Car): Street parking (restricted)
Parking (Coach/Bus): Layton Road car park
Police Force and Tel No: Metropolitan (020 8577 1212)
Disabled Visitors' Facilities:
Wheelchairs: Braemar Road
Blind: Commentary available
Anticipated Development(s): It is reported that the club wishes to relocate to the Feltham Arena where a new 15,000 all-seater stadium would be constructed costing some £20 million. There is, however, no confirmed schedule for this work and the club faces potential opposition from QPR who are also reported to be interested in this west London site.

KEY

C Club Offices
S Club Shop
E Entrance(s) for visiting supporters
R Refreshment bars for visiting supporters
T Toilets for visiting supporters

↑ North direction (approx)

❶ Ealing Road
❷ Braemar Road
❸ Brook Road South
❹ To M4 (¼ mile) & South Ealing Tube Station(1 mile)
❺ Brentford BR Station
❻ To A315 High Street & Kew Bridge

A promising start to the season saw the Bees threaten a Play-Off position at the very worst. Unfortunately, however, the Ron Noades/Ray Lewington combination was not sufficient to bring the team long-term success in the Second Division and a dramatic decline in form saw the team plummet down the table, with the team ultimately finishing a highly disappointing 17th. Whilst in 1999/2000 the team was never a serious relegation candidate, unless form picks up rapidly in 2000/01, fans will be seriously worried that a return to the Third Division beckons.

BRIGHTON & HOVE ALBION

Withdean Stadium, Tongdean Lane, Brighton BN1

Tel No: 01273 778855
Fax: 01273 321095
Advance Ticket Tel No: 01273 776992
Web Site: www.seagulls.co.uk
League: 3rd Division
Brief History: Founded 1900 as Brighton & Hove Rangers, changed to Brighton & Hove Albion 1902. Former grounds: Home Farm (Withdean), County Ground, Goldstone Ground (1902-1997), Priestfield Stadium (ground share with Gillingham) 1997-1999; moved to Withdean Stadium 1999. Founder members of the 3rd Division 1920. Record attendance (at Goldstone Ground): 36,747.
(Total) Current Capacity: c7,000
Visiting Supporters' Allocation: 325 (North Stand) (min)
Club Colours: Blue and white striped shirts, blue shorts
Nearest Railway Station: Preston Park
Parking (Cars): Street parking in the immediate vicinity of the ground is residents' only. This will be strictly enforced and it is suggested that intending visitors should use parking facilities away from the ground and use the proposed park and ride bus services that will be provided.
Parking (Coach/Bus): As directed
Police Force and Tel No: Sussex (01273 778922)
Disabled Visitors' Facilities
  Wheelchairs: Facilities in both North and South stands
  Blind: No special facility
Anticipated Development(s): Towards the end of June it was announced that the club had been granted permission to remain at Withdean for a further two years, up to the end of the 2002/03 season. This potentially coincides quite well with the proposed development of the new stadium at Village Way North, Falmer, which is expected to be completed for the start of the 2003/04 season. The new ground will have a 25,000 all-seated capacity.

KEY

Club Address:
  18 Queen's Road, Brighton, BN1 3XG.
  Tel: 01273 778855
  Fax: 01273 321095

Shop Address:
  6 Queen's Road, Brighton

⬆ North direction (approx)

Note: All games at Withdean will be all-ticket with no cash admissions on the day.

❶ Withdean Stadium
❷ London-Brighton railway line
❸ London Road (A23)
❹ Tongdean Lane
❺ Valley Drive
❻ To Brighton town centre and main railway station (1.75 miles)
❼ Tongdean Lane (with bridge under railway)
❽ South Stand
❾ A23 northwards to Crawley
❿ To Preston Park railway station
⓫ North Stand

Above: 684569; Right: 684566

Following the last couple of years when Brighton & Hove Albion have been more interested in the relegation battle from the Third Division into the Nationwide Conference than in events further up the table, 1999/2000 must have proved a surprise for fans of the Seagulls. No more last day traumas waiting on results as a position of mid-table security proved a triumph for Mickey Adams' team.

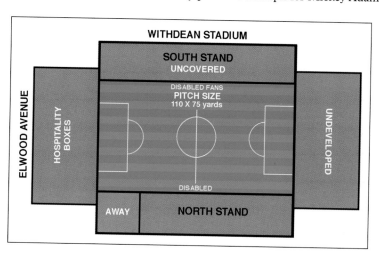

WITHDEAN STADIUM

SOUTH STAND
UNCOVERED

DISABLED FANS
PITCH SIZE
110 X 75 yards

ELWOOD AVENUE

HOSPITALITY BOXES

UNDEVELOPED

DISABLED

AWAY

NORTH STAND

BRISTOL CITY

Ashton Gate, Winterstoke Road, Ashton Road, Bristol BS3 2JE

Tel No: 0117 963 0630
Advance Tickets Tel No: 0117 966 6666
Fax: 0117 963 0700
Web Site: www.bcfc.co.uk
League: 2nd Division
Brief History: Founded 1894 as Bristol South End changed to Bristol City in 1897. Former Ground: St John's Lane, Bedminster, moved to Ashton Gate in 1904. Record attendance 43,445
(Total) Current Capacity: 21,200 (all seated)
Visiting Supporters' Allocation: 2,500 in Wedlock End (all seated; can be increased to 5,500 if necessary)
Club Colours: Red shirts, red shorts
Nearest Railway Station: Bristol Temple Meads

Parking (Car): Street parking
Parking (Coach/Bus): Marsh Road
Police Force and Tel No: Avon/Somerset (0117 927 7777)
Disabled Visitors' Facilities:
  Wheelchairs: Advanced notice not required
  Blind: Commentary available
Future Development(s): There are plans for the redevelopment of Ashton Gate, starting off with the construction of a new 12,000-seat stand to replace the existing Brunel Williams Stand. However, there are now also proposals for the construction of a brand new 36,000-seat stadium at Hengrove Park.

KEY

C Club Offices
S Club Shop
E Entrance(s) for visiting supporters

↑ North direction (approx)

❶ A370 Ashton Road
❷ A3209 Winterstoke Road
❸ To Temple Meads Station (1½ miles
❹ To City Centre, A4, M32 & M4
❺ Database Wedlock Stand
❻ Atyeo Stand

Following a disastrous campaign in the First Division in 1998/99, which saw John Ward replaced by Benny Lennartsson, fans of City were expecting great things from their team in 1999/2000 under the management of Tony Pulis. Pulis, whose previous team (Gillingham) had been unlucky to lose in the Play-Off final against Manchester City at the end of the previous season, brought to Ashton Gate a successful track record. With the team widely expected to make the Play-Offs at the very least, ninth place, some 18 points off the all-important sixth spot, can be regarded as a disappointment. Looking back at the 1999/2000 season, if one factor can be regarded as the major determinant for the club's failure to reach higher, it was the fact that, during the course of the season, City drew 19 games — more than any other team in the Nationwide League (with the exception of West Brom who also hit 19 draws) — with only 12 defeats. In 2000/01, the club can again look forward to derbies against Rovers, but fans will be expecting the team to emulate their local rivals and threaten the Play-Offs at the worst.

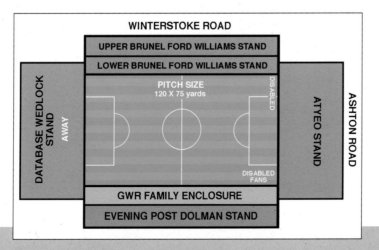

BRISTOL ROVERS

The Memorial Stadium, Filton Avenue, Horfield, Bristol BS7 0AQ

Registered Office: The Beeches, Broomhill Road, Brislington, Bristol BS4 5BF
Tel No: 0117 924 7474
Advance Tickets Tel No: 0117 924 3200
Fax: 0117 924 4454
Web Site: http://www.bristolrovers.co.uk
E-Mail: webmaster@bristolrovers.co.uk
League: 2nd Division
Brief History: Founded 1883 as Black Arabs, changed to Eastville Rovers (1884), Bristol Eastville Rovers (1896) and Bristol Rovers (1897). Former grounds: Purdown, Three Acres, The Downs (Horfield), Ridgeway, Bristol Stadium (Eastville), Twerton Park (1986-96), moved to The Memorial Ground 1996. Record attendance: (Eastville) 38,472, (Twerton Park) 9,813, (Memorial Ground) 9,274
(Total) Current Capacity: 11,917 (4,000 seated); standing capacity of 8,000 includes 500 on the Family Terrace

Visiting Supporters' Allocation: 1,132 (Centenary Stand Terrace)
Club Colours: Blue and white quartered shirts, white shorts
Nearest Railway Station: Filton or Stapleton Road
Parking (Car): Limited parking at ground for home fans only; street parking also available
Parking (Coach/Bus): As directed
Police Force and Tel No: Avon/Somerset (0117 927 7777)
Disabled Visitors' Facilities:
  Wheelchairs: 35 wheelchair positions
  Blind: Limited provision
Anticipated Development(s): Although work has been completed on the temporary structures at the Scoreboard and Terrace ends, the club's intention remains to construct a 20,000 all-seater stadium at the ground in the long term. There are proposals for the construction of a further temporary stand in the southwest corner of the ground.

KEY

C Rugby Club offices
E Entrance(s) for visiting supporters
R Refrshments for visiting supporters
T Toilets for visiting supporters

↑ North direction (approx)

❶ Filton Avenue
❷ Gloucester Road
❸ Muller Road
❹ To Bristol city centre (2.5 miles) and BR Temple Meads station (3 miles)
❺ Downer Road
❻ Car Park
❼ To M32 J2 (1.5 miles)
❽ Strathmore Road
❾ To Filton (1.5 miles)
❿ Centenary Stand
⓫ West Stand

Above: 684922; Right: 684914

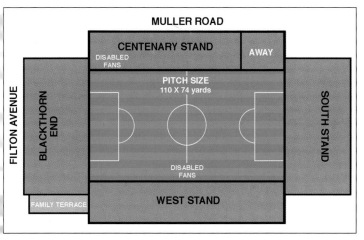

For much of the season, Rovers were in one of the two automatic promotion spots from the Second to First Division. However, a late season loss of form saw the team not only miss out on automatic promotion but also fail to make the Play-Offs. Defeat at already relegated Cardiff City on the last day of the season combined with Millwall's victory over Oxford United meant that the London team leapfrogged Rovers into the Play-Offs. Another season of local derbies against City in the Second Division are probably poor reward for a team that seemed destined for higher things during the 1999/2000 season.

BURNLEY

Turf Moor, Brunshaw Road, Burnley, Lancs, BB10 4BX

Tel No: 01282 700000
Advance Tickets Tel No: 01282 700010
Fax: 01282 700014
Web Site: www.clarets.co.uk
E-Mail: info@clarets.net
League: 2nd Division
Brief History: Founded 1882, Burnley Rovers (Rugby Club) combined with another Rugby Club, changed to soccer and name to Burnley. Moved from Calder Vale to Turf Moor in 1882. Founder-members Football League (1888). Record attendance 54,775
(Total) Current Capacity: 22,524 (all seated)
Visiting Supporters' Allocation: 4,125 (all seated in Cricket Field Stand)
Club Colours: Claret with blue sleeved shirts, white with claret and blue trim shorts
Nearest Railway Station: Burnley Central
Parking (Car): Church Street and Fulledge Rec.

(car parks)
Parking (Coach/Bus): As directed by Police
Police Force and Tel No: Lancashire (01282 425001)
Disabled Visitors' Facilities:
  Wheelchairs: Places available in North, East and Cricket Field stands
  Blind: Headsets provided with commentary
Anticipated Development(s): In conjunction with the adjacent Cricket Club, Burnley is proposing a redevelopment of the Cricket Field Stand, which would then be reallocated to home supporters. This would be followed, probably, by a redevelopment of the Bob Lord Stand with the intention of raising the ground's capacity significantly above the current 22,524. There is, however, no schedule for this work, much of which depends upon the financial position of the Cricket Club.

KEY

C Club Offices
S Club Shop
E Entrance(s) for visiting supporters

⬆ North direction (approx)

❶ Brunshaw Road
❷ Belvedere Road
❸ Burnley Central BR Station (¹/₂ mile)
❹ Cricket Ground
❺ Cricket Field Stand
❻ East (Jimmy McIlroy) Stand
❼ Bob Lord Stand
❽ North (James Hargreaves) Stand

Historically, one of the great names of English football, Burnley have languished in the lower divisions for more years than their fans would like. Manager Stan Ternent moved to the club for the 1998/99 season following the club's flirtation with relegation the previous season under Chris Waddle, but the experienced manager brought no success in his first season. As a result, fans were lukewarm towards him at the start of the 1999/2000 campaign. In the event, a late run saw the team move through the Play-Off zone and into the second automatic promotion spot behind already promoted Preston North End with a last day victory over relegated Scunthorpe and Gillingham's defeat at Wrexham. Fans will, no doubt, be hoping that Burnley can stay in the First Division for longer than the previous Lancashire team — Bury — managed.

BURY

Gigg Lane, Bury, Lancashire, BL9 9HR

Tel No: 0161 764 4881
Advance Tickets Tel No: 0161 705 2144
Fax: 0161 764 5521
Web Site: www.buryfc.co.uk
E-Mail: buryfc@dial.pipex.com
League: 2nd Division
Brief History: Founded 1885, no former names or former grounds. Record attendance 35,000
(Total) Current Capacity: 12,500 (all seated)
Visiting Supporters' Allocation: 2,676 (all seated) in West Stand
Club Colours: White shirts, royal blue shorts
Nearest Railway Station: Bury Interchange

Parking (Car): Street parking
Parking (Coach/Bus): As directed by Police
Police Force and Tel No: Greater Manchester (0161 872 5050)
Disabled Visitors' Facilities:
  Wheelchairs: South Stand (home) and West Stand (away)
  Blind: Commentary available
Anticipated Development(s): The completion of the rebuilt Cemetery End means that current plans for the redevelopment of Gigg Lane have been completed.

KEY

C Club Offices
S Club Shop
E Entrance(s) for visiting supporters

⬆ North direction (approx)

❶ Car Park
❷ Gigg Lane
❸ A56 Manchester Road
❹ Town Centre & Bury Interchange (Metrolink) (³/₄ mile)
❺ West (Manchester Road) Stand
❻ Cemetery End

Above: 684931; Right: 684926

GIGG LANE

MAIN STAND

PITCH SIZE
112 X 72 yards

MANCHESTER ROAD

WEST STAND
AWAY

DISABLED
FANS

CEMETERY END
STAND

DISABLED FANS

SOUTH STAND
MILLIKEN ENCLOSURE

Relegated back to the Second Division after two seasons in the First, the Shakers were widely predicted to struggle even in the lower division and, in this, fans were right to be pessimistic. Located in the bottom half of the division for much of the season, the now departed Neil Warnock's team never looked like serious candidates to threaten for a Play-Off spot at the very least; indeed, for a time, it appeared that the club was more likely to feature in the battle at the wrong end of the table. A position of mid-table anonymity offers the potential for a determined push towards promotion in 2000/01 but the prospect of a return to First Division football at the modernised Gigg Lane looks unlikely in the near future.

CAMBRIDGE UNITED

Abbey Stadium, Newmarket Road, Cambridge, CB5 8LN

Tel No: 01223 566500
Advance Tickets Tel No: 01223 566500
Fax: 01223 566502
Web Site: www.cambridgeunited.com
League: 2nd Division
Brief History: Founded 1913 as Abbey United, changed to Cambridge United in 1951. Former Grounds: Midsummer Common, Stourbridge Common, Station Farm Barnwell (The Celery Trenches) & Parker's Piece, moved to Abbey Stadium in 1933. Record attendance 14,000
(Total) Current Capacity: 9,247 (3,198 seated)
Visiting Supporters' Allocation: 2,272 (322 seated)
Club Colours: Amber and black shirts, amber shorts
Nearest Railway Station: Cambridge (2 miles)
Parking (Car): Coldhams Common

Parking (Coach/Bus): Coldhams Common
Police Force and Tel No: Cambridge (01223 358966)
Disabled Visitors' Facilities:
  Wheelchairs: Limited number that should be pre-booked
  Blind: No special facility
Anticipated Development(s): There are plans to construct a new 3,000-seat stand at the North End, with a planning application recently made. If work does progress, then home fans will be relocated to the South Terrace (currently occupied by away fans) with a consequent reduction in the allocation to away fans to just 322 in the Habbin Stand. Once work on the new North Stand is completed, attention will turn to the South Terrace.

KEY
C Club Offices
S Club Shop
E Entrance(s) for visiting supporters
R Refreshment bars for visiting supporters
T Toilets for visiting supporters

↑ North direction (approx)

❶ A1134 Newmarket Road
❷ To A11 for Newmarket
❸ To City Centre, Cambridge BR Station (2 miles) and M11
❹ Whitehill Road

Above: 614421; Right: 614415

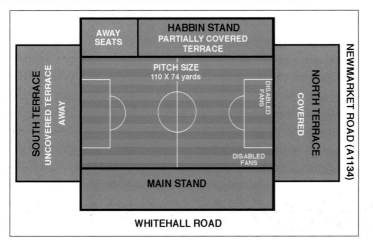

AWAY
SEATS

HABBIN STAND
PARTIALLY COVERED
TERRACE

SOUTH TERRACE
UNCOVERED TERRACE
AWAY

PITCH SIZE
110 X 74 yards

DISABLED
FANS

NORTH TERRACE
COVERED

NEWMARKET ROAD (A1134)

DISABLED
FANS

MAIN STAND

WHITEHALL ROAD

Promoted at the end of end of 1998/99, when the team finished as runners-up to champions Brentford in the Third Division, many expected Cambridge United to maintain their upwardly mobile lifestyle and threaten the promotion places in Division Two. In the event, Roy McFarland's team was involved in a desperate struggle in 1999/2000, but at the wrong end of the table. In the relegation zone for much of the season, the team was eventually to finish four points and two places above the drop, despite a last day defeat at home by Wycombe Wanderers.

CARDIFF CITY

Ninian Park, Sloper Road, Cardiff, CF1 8SX

Tel No: 01222 221001
Advance Tickets Tel No: 01222 222857
Fax: 01222 341148
Web Site: www.cardiffcity.fc.co.uk
E-mail: ccafc@baynet.co.uk
League: 3rd Division
Brief History: Founded 1899. Former Grounds: Riverside Cricket Club, Roath, Sophia Gardens, Cardiff Arms Park and The Harlequins Rugby Ground, moved to Ninian Park in 1910. Ground record attendance 61,566 (Wales v. England, 1961)
(Total) Current Capacity: 16,047 (12,647 seated)
Visiting Supporters' Allocation: 4,478 (1,078 seated in Grandstand Blocks A-B; 3,400 in Grangetown Terrace)
Club Colours: Blue shirts, white shorts
Nearest Railway Station: Ninian Park

(adjacent) (Cardiff Central 1 mile)
Parking (Car): Opposite Ground, no street parking around ground
Parking (Coach/Bus): Sloper Road
Police Force and Tel No: South Wales (01222 222111)
Disabled Visitors' Facilities:
Wheelchairs: Corner Canton Stand/Popular Bank (covered)
Blind: No special facility
Anticipated Development(s): Work has been undertaken at the Grangetown End in order to improve facilities on the open terrace. The next stage of work at the ground is likely to be the insertion of seats on the open paddock in front of the Popular Bank Stand. There are still rumours of a possible relocation, although nothing is confirmed at the current time.

KEY

C Club Offices

S Club Shop

E Entrance(s) for visiting supporters

R Refreshment bars for visiting supporters

T Toilets for visiting supporters (Terrace only, when used)

↑ North direction (approx)

❶ Sloper Road
❷ B4267 Leckwith Road
❸ Car Park
❹ To A4232 & M4 Junction 33 (8 miles)
❺ Ninian Park Road
❻ To City Centre & Cardiff Central BR Station (1 mile)
❼ To A48 Western Avenue, A49M, and M4 Junction 32 and 29
❽ Ninian Park BR station

Above: 684942; Right: 684936

It is a sad fact that there is an increasing gulf between all the divisions and not just between the First Division and the Premier League. One of a number of teams to struggle after being promoted, Cardiff City were one of two of the promoted teams at the end of the 1998/99 season to face an immediate return to the Third Division at the end of 1999/2000. The team's failure to build upon the success of promotion is made all the more galling by the fact that fellow Welsh team Swansea City will be one of those replacing them in the Second Division in 2000/01.

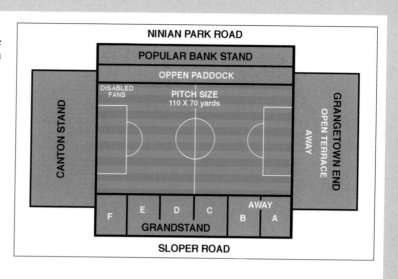

CARLISLE UNITED

Brunton Park, Warwick Road, Carlisle, CA1 1LL

Tel No: 01228 526237
Advance Tickets Tel No: 01228 526237
Fax: 01228 530138
E-Mail: www.carlisleunited.co.uk
Website: www.carlisleunited.co.uk
League: 3rd Division
Brief History: Founded 1904 as Carlisle United (previously named Shaddongate United). Former Grounds: Millholme Bank and Devonshire Park, moved to Brunton Park in 1909. Record attendance 27,500
(Total) Current Capacity: 16,500 (7,209 seated)
Visiting Supporters' Allocation: 2,000 (East Stand blocks 1 to 4)

Club Colours: Royal blue shirts, blue shorts
Nearest Railway Station: Carlisle Citadel
Parking (Car): Rear of ground
Parking (Coach/Bus): St Aiden's Road car park
Police Force and Tel No: Cumbria (01228 28191)
Disabled Visitors' Facilities:
  Wheelchairs: East Stand and Paddock (prior arrangement)
  Blind: No special facilities
Anticipated Development(s): Long term plans for a 28,000 all-seater stadium, but nothing concrete planned after completion of the new East Stand

KEY

C Club Offices
E Entrance(s) for visiting supporters
R Refreshment bars for visiting supporters
T Toilets for visiting supporters

↑ North direction (approx)

❶ A69 Warwick Road
❷ To M6 Junction 43
❸ Carlisle Citadel BR Station (1 mile)
❹ Greystone Road
❺ Car Park
❻ Petteril End (closed)

Another last day escape saw Carlisle United preserve its Nationwide League status for another season. One of a trio of teams — the others being Chester City and Shrewsbury Town — that faced relegation to the Conference on the last day, United survived, despite being beaten 1-0 by Brighton & Hove Albion (ironically a team also noted as escapologists — witness the victory over Hereford some years back). Results elsewhere meant that Chester were relegated and Carlisle live to battle another season. Some years back chairman Michael Knighton prophesied that within 10 years the team would be in the Premier League; with time running out it looks as though his grand plan is more appropriate to keeping the team in the nether regions of the Third Division than bringing Manchester United to Brunton Park. Will 2000/01 be the season that the team's luck finally runs out? Whatever happens in the new season, it will be without Knighton at the helm; shortly after the end of 1999/2000 it was announced that he was standing down as chairman.

CHARLTON ATHLETIC

The Valley, Floyd Road, Charlton, London, SE7 8BL

Tel No: 020 833 4000
Advance Tickets Tel No: 020 8333 4010
Fax: 020 8333 4001
Web Site: http:/www.cafc.co.uk
E-Mail: contact@cafc.co.uk
League: FA Premier
Brief History: Founded 1905. Former grounds: Siemens Meadows, Woolwich Common, Pound Park, Angerstein Athletic Ground, The Mount Catford, Selhurst Park (Crystal Palace FC), Boleyn Ground (West Ham United FC), The Valley (1912-23, 1924-85, 1992-date). Founder Members 3rd Division South. Record attendance 75,031
(Total) Current Capacity: 20,043 (all seated)
Visiting Supporters' Allocation: 2,000 (all seated in South Stand)
Club Colours: Red shirts, white shorts
Nearest Railway Station: Charlton

Parking (Car): Street parking
Parking (Coach/Bus): As directed by Police
Police Force and Tel No: Metropolitan (020 8853 8212)
Disabled Visitors' Facilities:
  Wheelchairs: East/West/South stands
  Blind: Commentary, 12 spaces
Anticipated Development(s): Although there was talk last year that the club might relocate from The Valley to a proposed new ground at the Millennium Dome. It is now confirmed that the club has pulled out of a consortium for this in favour of further worth at The Valley. Planning permission has been granted for work on an expanded North Stand and work is expected to start on this in early 2001 with an expected completion date for it to be brought into use at the start of the 2001/02 season.

KEY

C Club Offices
E Entrance(s) for visiting supporters
R Refreshment bars for visiting supporters
T Toilets for visiting supporters

↑ North Direction (approx)

❶ Harvey Gardens
❷ A206 Woolwich Road
❸ Valley Grove
❹ Floyd Road
❺ Charlton BR Station
❻ River Thames
❼ Thames Barrier
❽ West stand
❾ South stand (away)
❿ Charlton Church Lane
⓫ Charlton Lane

Above: 679520; *Right:* 679515

Relegated back to the First Division, after one season in the Premier League, in 1998/99, under the astute management of Alan Curbishley, Charlton stormed to the First Division title and, with it, renewed membership of the top flight of English football. A long winning streak in mid-season saw the club establish a commanding lead, although several lacklustre performances towards the end of the season meant that confirmation of the team's promotion was delayed. The champions of 1998/99 — Sunderland — established themselves well in the Premier League in 1999/2000 and Charlton fans will certainly be hoping that their team can emulate this success rather than the fate of most other teams promoted from the First Division.

WOOLWICH ROAD
FLOYD ROAD

UPPER LOWER

R	Q	P	N	M	L	K	J
H	G	F	E	D	C	B	A

UPPER WEST
LOWER WEST
DISABLED

PITCH SIZE
112 X 73 yards

A	B	C	D	E	F	G	H

DISABLED
EAST STAND

CHARLTON LANE

VALLEY GROVE (DEAD END)
(JIMMY SEED) SOUTH STAND
G H A B C D E F
G H J K L F E D C B A

HARVEY GARDENS
NORTH STAND
F E D C B A

CHELSEA

Stamford Bridge, Fulham Road, London, SW6 1HS

Tel No: 020 7385 5545
Advance Tickets Tel No: 020 7386 7799
Fax: 020 7384 4831
Web Site: www.chelseafc.co.uk
League: F.A. Premier
Brief History: Founded 1905. Admitted to Football League (2nd Division) on formation. Stamford Bridge venue for F.A. Cup Finals 1919-22. Record attendance 82,905
(Total) Current Capacity: 35,436 (all seated)
Visiting Supporters' Allocation: Approx. 1,600 (East Stand Lower; can be increased to 3,200 if required)
Club Colours: Blue shirts, blue shorts
Nearest Railway Station: Fulham Broadway or West Brompton

Parking (Car): Street parking
Parking (Coach/Bus): As directed by Police
Police Force and Tel No: Metropolitan (020 7385 1212)
Disabled Visitors' Facilities:
  Wheelchairs: East Stand
  Blind: No special facility
Anticipated Development(s): Following a lengthy dispute with the planning authorities, Chelsea has now been granted permission to complete the second tier and roof of the West Stand and work started on this project in mid-2000. Once completed, this will take the capacity of Stamford Bridge to 42,000.

KEY

⬆ North direction (approx)

❶ A308 Fulham Road
❷ Central London
❸ To Fulham Broadway Tube Station
❹ Mathew Harding Stand
❺ East Stand
❻ West Stand (to be completed)
❼ South (Shed) Stand
❽ West Brompton Station

Above: 685823; Right: 685831

Most Chelsea fans will regard the 1999/2000 season as being a curate's egg; success in reaching the quarter finals of the Champions League and winning the FA Cup offset against a number of poor performances in the Premier League, which resulted in the team finishing in fifth place and thus not qualifying for the Champions League in 2000/01. With a team rich in talent, much of it from overseas — indeed Chelsea on occasion were able to field a team devoid of players qualified to play for any of the home countries — a number of the team's high profile (and expensive) stars failed to fire on all cylinders. The team's only triumph came in the last FA Cup final to be played at Wembley before the ground's redevelopment; unfortunately, the game failed to live up to expectations, with Chelsea defeating Aston Villa by a single goal. With a place assured in the 2000/01 UEFA Cup, it is probable that the forecast breaking up of the team may be delayed, although a number of the foreign stars are likely to have played their last game for the team.

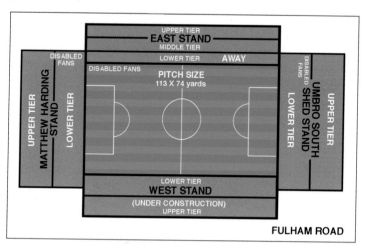

CHELTENHAM TOWN

Whaddon Road, Cheltenham, Gloucestershire GL52 5NA

Tel No: 01242 573558
Advance Tickets Tel No: 01242 573558
Fax: 01242 224675
Web Site: www.cheltenhamtown.co.uk
E-Mail: office@cheltenhamtown-co.uk
League: 3rd Divison
Brief History: Cheltenham Town was founded in 1892. It moved to Whaddon Road in 1932 having previously played at Carter's Field. After two seasons in the Conference it achieved Nationwide League status at the end of the 1998/99 season. Record attendance 8,326
(Total) Current Capacity: 6,114 (1,088 seated)
Visiting Supporters' Allocation: 1,470 (maximum comprising 720 in Whaddon Road Terrace – uncovered – and 750 in Wymans Road Stand
Club Colours: Red and white striped shirts, red shorts

Nearest Railway Station: Cheltenham (1.5 miles)
Parking (Car): Limited parking at ground; otherwise on-street
Parking (Coach/Bus): As directed by Police
Police Force and Tel No: Gloucestershire (01242 521321)
Disabled Visitors' Facilities:
  Wheelchairs: Six spaces in front of Main Stand
  Blind: No special facility
Anticipated Development(s): The improvements to the Main Stand were completed during the course of the 1999/2000 season. The Prestbury Road End was covered during summer 2000. The club's policy remains to follow this work with attention to the Wymans Road Stand.

KEY
C Club Offices
E Entrance(s) for visiting supporters

↑ North direction (approx)

❶ B4632 Prestbury Road
❷ Cromwell Road
❸ Whaddon Road
❹ Wymans Road
❺ To B4075 Priors Road
❻ To B4075 Prior Road
❼ To Cheltenham town centre and railway station (1.5 and 2 miles respectively)
❽ Main Stand
❾ Wymans Road Stand
❿ Prestbury Road End
⓫ Whaddon Road End

Above: 684954; *Right:* 684947

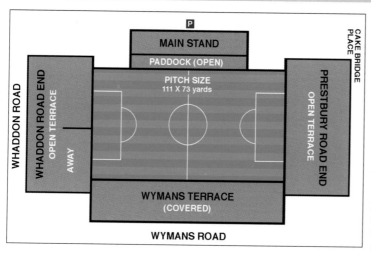

WHADDON ROAD

WHADDON ROAD END
OPEN TERRACE

AWAY

P

MAIN STAND

PADDOCK (OPEN)

PITCH SIZE
111 X 73 yards

PRESTBURY ROAD END
OPEN TERRACE

CAKE BRIDGE
PLACE

WYMANS TERRACE
(COVERED)

WYMANS ROAD

The Robins initially found the transition from Nationwide Conference to Nationwide League to be difficult and it took some weeks for the team to find its feet at the higher level. As the season progressed, however, Steve Cotterill's team gradually moved up the table and, for a period, a Play-Off spot appeared to be a real possibility. In the event, defeat on the last day away at Southend coupled with Hartlepool's 3-0 win at Hull meant that the Tees-side team took the fourth Play-Off spot and resulted in Cheltenham finishing eighth. The new season will see fans hoping that the Robins can go further and reach the Play-Offs at the very least.

CHESTERFIELD

Recreation Ground, Saltergate, Chesterfield, S40 4SX

Tel No: 01246 209765
Advance Tickets Tel No: 01246 209765
Fax: 01246 556799
Web Site: http://www.spireites.com
League: 3rd Division
Brief History: Found 1886. Former Ground: Spital Vale. Formerly named Chesterfield Town. Record attendance 30,968
(Total) Current Capacity: 8,960 (2,674 seated)
Visiting Supporters' Allocation: 2,528 (458 seated)
Club Colours: Blue shirts, blue shorts
Nearest Railway Station: Chesterfield
Parking (Car): Saltergate car park, street parking

Parking (Coach/Bus): As directed by Police
Police Force and Tel No: Derbyshire (01246 220100)
Disabled Visitors' Facilities:
   Wheelchairs: Saltergate Stand
   Blind: No special facility
Anticipated Development(s): Plans for the relocation of the club continue. However, given the fact that the proposed new stadium will have a capacity of 10-12,000 — as opposed to just under 9,000 at Saltergate — there is understandable doubt as to whether this work will progress. There remains no confirmed schedule for this work.

KEY

C Club Offices
S Club Shop
E Entrance(s) for visiting supporters
R Refreshment bars for visiting supporters
T Toilets for visiting supporters

↑ North direction (approx)

❶ Saltergate
❷ Cross Street
❸ St Margaret's Drive
❹ West Bars
❺ To A617 & M1 Junction 29
❻ To station and town centre
❼ A619 Markham Road

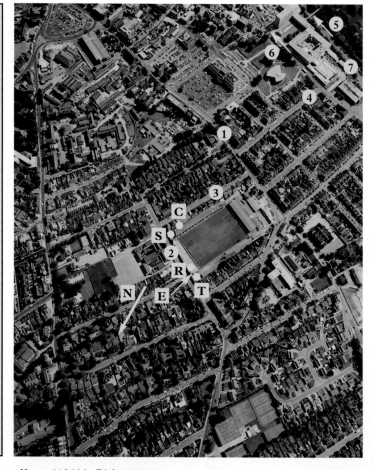

Above: 612683; Right: 612687

Adrift at the bottom of the Second Division for much of the season, it came as no surprise when John Duncan, the manager who had led Chesterfield to inspired cup performances in 1997/98, was shown the door, to be replaced by Nicky Law. However, the Spireites failed to fulfil the pre-season expectations of another season of mid-table mediocrity and finished the season rooted to the Second Division's basement. New manager Nicky Law will take over a team relegated to the Third Division with the expectation amongst fans that the team can bounce back immediately from the set-back.

COLCHESTER UNITED

Layer Road Ground, Colchester, CO2 7JJ

Tel No: 01206 508800
Advance Tickets Tel No: 01206 508802
Fax: 01206 508803
Web Site: http://www.cufc.co.uk
League: 2nd Division
Brief History: Founded 1937, joined Football
League 1950, relegated 1990, promoted 1992.
Record attendance 19,072
(Total) Current Capacity: 7,556 (1,877
seated)
Visiting Supporters' Allocation: 1,342
Club Colours: Royal blue and white shirts, blue
shorts
Nearest Railway Station: Colchester Town
Parking (Car): Street parking
Parking (Coach/Bus): Boadicea Way

Police Force and Tel No: Essex (01206 762212)
Disabled Visitors' Facilities:
Wheelchairs: Space for six in front of terrace
(next to Main Stand)
Blind: Space for 3 blind persons and 3 guides
(two regularly occupied by home supporters)
Anticipated Development(s): In early 1998
the club, in conjunction with the local council,
undertook a feasibility study into whether it
was feasible to develop Layer Road or whether
a new stadium should be built. Consultants in
early 1999 suggested the construction of a new
10,000-seat stadium, possibly at Stanhope.
However, no definite plans for this work have
been announced, and expect United to remain
at Layer Road for at least another season.

KEY

C Club Offices

S Club Shop

E Entrance(s) for visiting
supporters

R Refreshment bars for visiting
supporters

T Toilets for visiting supporters

↑ North direction (approx)

❶ B1026 Layer Road
❷ Town Centre & Colchester
Town BR Station (2 miles)
❸ Main Stand
❹ Popular Side
❺ Clock Street End

Hovering around the relegation zone for all the 1999/2000 season, last year was not one of significant progress for United — given the fact that the team finished 18th at the end of 1998/99 and 18th and the end of 1999/2000 it could be argued that the team made no progress at all, I suppose. Manager Mick Wadworth was not flavour of season for many Us' fans, given that he disposed of many favourites, and it is hard to see the new season as providing anything other than another year of struggle for the team.

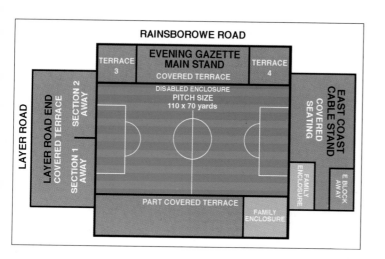

COVENTRY CITY

Highfield Stadium, King Richard Street, Coventry CV2 4FW

Tel No: 02476 234000
Advance Tickets Tel No: 02476 234020
Fax: 02476 234009
Web Site: www.ccfc.co.uk
E-Mail: info@ccfc.co.uk
League: F.A. Premier
Brief History: Founded 1883 as Singers F.C., changed name to Coventry City in 1898. Former grounds: Dowell's Field, Stoke Road Ground, moved to Highfield Road in 1899. Record attendance 51,455
(Total) Current Capacity: 23,673 all seated
Visiting Supporters' Allocation: 4,148 all seated in Mitchells & Butler Stand
Club Colours: Sky blue and white stripe shirts, white and sky blue shorts

Nearest Railway Station: Coventry
Parking (Car): Street parking
Parking (Coach/Bus): Gosford Green Coach Park
Police Force and Tel No: West Midlands (02476 539010)
Disabled Visitors' Facilities:
   Wheelchairs: Clock Stand and East Stand
   Blind: Clock Stand (booking necessary)
Anticipated Development(s): Despite the expenditure on Highfield Road in recent years, the club has announced that it intends to build a new 40,000-seat stadium at Foleshill. As yet there is no definite time scale for the proposed move but opening is planned for the start of the 2002/03 season.

KEY

C Club Offices
S Club Shop
E Entrance(s) for visiting supporters
R Refreshment bars for visiting supporters
T Toilets for visiting supporters

↑ North direction (approx)

❶ Swan Lane
❷ A4600 Walsgrave Road
❸ Thackhall Street
❹ Coventry BR Station (1 mile)
❺ To M6 Junction 2 and M69
❻ To M45 Junction 1
❼ Gosford Green Coach Park

Curiously, Coventry City managed a season where the club's Premier League survival was rarely in doubt. Despite this, however, the team managed never to win an away game all season and, without the strong performances at Highfield Road, the team could well have been sucked into the relegation quagmire. During the course of the season Gordon Strachan strengthened the team with quality players like Robbie Keane from Wolves as well as the two Moroccans, but failure to win away from home bodes ill for the future. With the 2000/01 Premier League likely to be stronger than that in 1999/2000, fans of the Sky Blues will have to hope that the team's travel sickness does not turn into a terminal malaise.

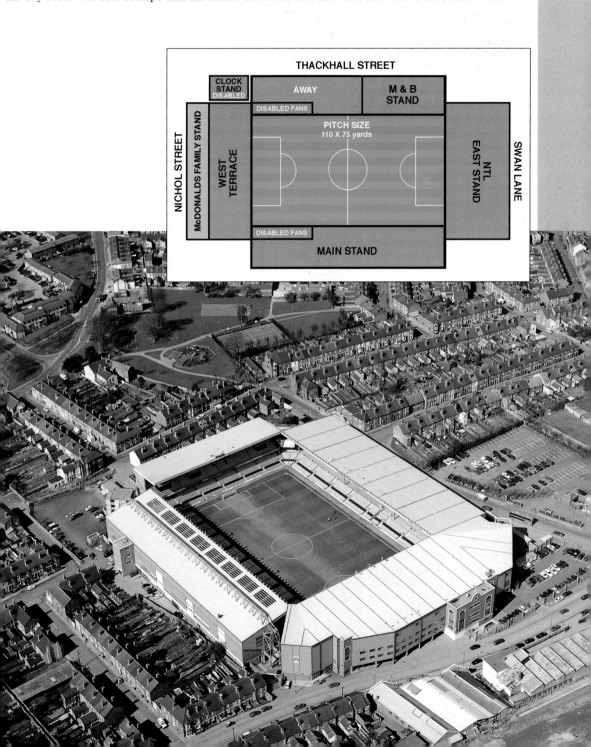

CREWE ALEXANDRA

Gresty Road Ground, Crewe, Cheshire, CW2 6EB

Tel No: 01270 213014
Advance Tickets Tel No: 01270 252610
Fax: 01270 216320
League: 1st Division
Brief History: Founded 1877. Former Grounds: Alexandra Recreation Ground (Nantwich Road), Earle Street Cricket Ground, Edleston Road, Old Sheds Fields, Gresty Road (Adjacent to current Ground), moved to current Ground in 1906. Founder members of 2nd Division (1892) until 1896. Founder members of 3rd Division North (1921). Record attendance 20,000
(Total) Current Capacity: 10,100 all seated
Visiting Supporters' Allocation: 1,736 (BMW Stand)
Club Colours: Red shirts, navy blue shorts
Nearest Railway Station: Crewe

Parking (car): There is a car park adjacent to the ground that is priced at £1.80 for eight hours. It should be noted that there is a residents' only scheme in operation in the streets surrounding the ground.
Parking (Coach/Bus): As directed by Police
Police Force and Tel No: Cheshire (01270 500222)
Disabled Visitors' Facilities:
　Wheelchairs: Available on all four sides
　Blind: Commentary available
Anticipated Development(s): The new main stand was completed for the 1999/2000 season, taking the ground's capacity to 10,000 — and very dramatic it looks too — and this marks the completion of current developments at Gresty Road.

KEY

C	Club Offices
S	Club Shop
E	Entrance(s) for visiting supporters

↑ North direction (approx)

❶ Crewe BR Station
❷ Gresty Road
❸ Gresty Road
❹ A534 Nantwich Road
❺ To A5020 to M6 Junction 16
❻ To M6 Junction 17 [follow directions at roundabout to M6 J16/J17]
❼ Main Stand
❽ Gresty Road (Adtranz) Stand
❾ Railway End
❿ Ringways Stand (BMW)(away)
⓫ Car Park

58

Above: 684966; *Right:* 684958

Although Dario Gradi's team flirted with the relegation places from the First Division for much of the season, the team managed to string together a good set of results towards the end of the term — including three wins and a draw in the last five games — which means that First Division football will grace Gresty Road again in 2000/01. The success of Crewe, considering its relatively limited resources, and the continuing faith in manager Gradi are aspects of the game that can inspire all teams. Now that Gresty Road's capacity has been increased, following the construction of the new stand, it is to be hoped that Alexandra will no longer need to sell such talented players as Seth Johnson and Gareth Whalley in the future in order to secure the team's survival. For fans, a position of mid-table security in 2000/01 will represent a considerable advance on two seasons of struggle against relegation.

RAILTRACK MAIN STAND
DISABLED FANS
PITCH SIZE
112 X 74 yards
ROLLS ROYCE & BENTLEY MOTORS FAMILY STAND
DISABLED FANS
DISABLED FANS
GRESTY ROAD (ADTRANZ) STAND
GRESTY ROAD
DISABLED FANS
BMW STAND
AWAY
P

CRYSTAL PALACE

Selhurst Park, London, SE25 6PU

Tel No: 020 8768 6000
Advance Tickets Tel No: 020 8771 8841
Fax: 020 8768 6114
Web Site: www.cpfc.co.uk
E-Mail: palace@cpfc.1.demon.co.uk
Ticket Office/Fax: 020 8653 4708
League: 1st Division
Brief History: Founded 1905. Former Grounds: The Crystal Palace (F.A. Cup Finals venue), London County Athletic Ground (Herne Hill), The Nest (Croydon Common Athletic Ground), moved to Selhurst Park in 1924. Founder members 3rd Division (1920). Record attendance 51,842
(Total) Current Capacity: 26,400 all seated
Visiting Supporters' Allocation: Approx 2,500 in Arthur Wait Stand
Club Colours: Blue and claret striped shirts, red shorts
Nearest Railway Station: Selhurst, Norwood Junction and Thornton Heath

Parking (Car): Street parking and Sainsbury's car park
Parking (Coach/Bus): Thornton Heath
Police Force and Tel No: Metropolitan (020 8653 8568)
Disabled Visitors' Facilities:
  Wheelchairs: Arthur Wait and Holmesdale Stands
  Blind: Commentary available
Anticipated Development(s): Planning permission has been obtained for the construction of a new Main Stand. As yet there is no confirmed start date. The take-over of the club by Michael Jordan has seen the new owners negotiate a 10-year lease with the Ron Noades-controlled company that owns Selhurst Park. Although too early to say at this stage, this may mean that planned development work will now progress.

KEY

C Club Offices
S Club Shop
E Entrance(s) for visiting supporters
T Toilets for visiting supporters

↑ North direction (approx)

❶ Whitehorse Lane
❷ Park Road
❸ A213 Selhurst Road
❹ Selhurst BR Station (1/2 mile)
❺ Norwood Junction BR Station (1/4 mile)
❻ Thornton Heath BR Station (1/2 mile)
❼ Car Park (Sainsbury's)

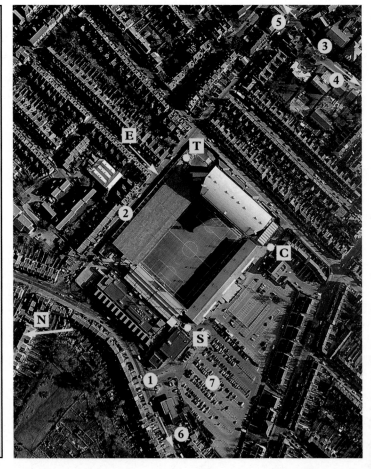

As far as fans of the Eagles are concerned, the club's survival is the biggest triumph of the season and Steve Coppell's success in keeping them in the First Division is an added bonus, given the team's financial liabilities. In administration since March 1999 as a result of the ill-fated efforts of Mark Goldberg, the team's mid-table position reflects greatly on the skills of Coppell in dealing with the difficult circumstances in which the club found itself and his squad of, largely, unknown talent. Looking to the new season, the arrival of new chairman Simon Jordan holds out the promise of a new start for the troubled club, although this will be without the influence of Coppell, who has now left the club.

MAIN STAND

PITCH SIZE
110 X74 yards

HOLMSDALE ROAD

HOLMSDALE ROAD STAND

DISABLED FANS

DISABLED FANS

AWAY

ARTHUR WAIT STAND

PARK ROAD

WHITEHORSE LANE

CROYDON ADVERTISER FAMILY STAND

DARLINGTON

Feethams Ground, Darlington, DL1 5JB

Tel No: 01325 240240
Advance Tickets Tel No: 01325 240240
Fax: 01325 240500
Web Site: www.darlingtonfc.net
League: 3rd Division
Brief History: Founded 1883. Founder
Members of 3rd Division North (1921),
Relegated from 4th Division (1989). Promoted
from GM Vauxhall Conference in 1990.
Record attendance 21,023
(Total) Current Capacity: 8,353 (4,053 seated)
Visiting Supporters' Allocation: 800 (200
seated)
Club Colours: White and black shirts, black
shorts
Nearest Railway Station: Darlington
Parking (Car): Street parking

Parking (Coach/Bus): As directed by Police
Police Force and Tel No: Durham (01325
467681)
Disabled Visitors' Facilities:
   Wheelchairs: 42 spaces available
   Blind: By prior arrangement
Anticipated Development(s): Despite recent
investment in Feethams — which the club only
rents — work started on a new £7.5 million
25,000-seat capacity ground at Neasham Road
in June 2000. It is expected that the new
ground will be opened during the course of the
2000/01 season. It is probable that Feethams
— on which considerable sums have been
spent in recent seasons — will be retained for
reserve team matches.

KEY

C Club Offices
S Club Shop
E Entrance(s) for visiting supporters
R Refreshment bars for visiting supporters
T Toilets for visiting supporters

↑ North direction (approx)

❶ Polam Lane
❷ Victoria Embankment
❸ Feethams Cricket Ground
❹ Victoria Road
❺ Darlington BR Station (¼ mile)
❻ To A1 (M)
❼ East Stand

Above: 680621; *Right:* 680619

In future years, quiz questions may ask 'which football team was defeated in the FA Cup twice in the same year's competition?' The answer is, of course, Darlington. The now departed David Hodgson's team was defeated in the second round and then benefited from Manchester United's withdrawal to get another opportunity of progressing in the cup. However, the club's reprieve was to be shortlived as third round defeat at Aston Villa saw the Quakers again eliminated. Better luck, however, marked the club's Third Division campaign, although the club was pipped at the post for the final automatic promotion place. Defeating local rivals Hartlepool in the Play-Off semi-final, the team faced Peterborough at Wembley and, unfortunately suffered a 1-0 reverse despite dominating much of the game. Under ambitious chairman George Reynolds, the Quakers are looking to go places; only time will tell if the club can fulfil these hopes or whether the Carlisle United syndrome is the result. Whatever happens, Third Division football will be the fare at Feethams again this season.

AWAY   WEST STAND

PITCH SIZE
112 X 74 yards

POLAM LANE

AWAY OVERSPILL

SOUTH END
UNCOVERED
TERRACE

DISABLED FANS

EAST STAND

TIN SHED
CRICKET GROUND
END

RIVER SKERNE

DERBY COUNTY

Pride Park, Derby, Derbyshire DE24 8XL

Tel No: 01332 202202
Advance Tickets Tel No: 01322 202909
Fax: 01322 667540
Web Site: www.dcfc.co.uk
E-Mail: press.office@dcfc.co.uk
League: F.A. Premiership
Brief History: Founded 1884. Former grounds: The Racecourse Ground, the Baseball Ground (1894-1997), moved to Pride Park 1997. Founder members of the Football League (1888). Record capacity at the Baseball Ground: 41,826; at Pride Park: 32,916
(Total) Current Capacity: 33,258
Visiting Supporters' Allocation: 4,800 in the South Stand
Club Colours: White shirts and black shorts

Nearest Railway Station: Derby
Parking (Car): 2,300 places at the ground designated for season ticket holders. Also two 1,000 car parks on the A6/A52 link road. No on-street parking
Parking (Coach/Bus): As directed
Police Force and Tel No: Derbyshire (01332 290100)
Disabled Visitors' Facilities:
  Wheelchairs: 70 home/30 away spaces
  Blind: Commentary available
Anticipated Development(s): There are no definite plans for the further development of Pride Park following the completion of the southwest corner.

KEY

C Club Offices
S Club Shop
E Entrance(s) for visiting supporters

↑ North direction (approx)

❶ To Derby Midland BR station
❷ North Stand
❸ West (Mansfield Bitter) Stand
❹ South Stand (away)
❺ East Stand
❻ Derwent Parade
❼ To A52/M1
❽ To City Centre and A6
❾ A52

Above: 679691; Right: 679687

A disappointing season for Jim Smith's Derby County saw the team involved in the dour struggle against the drop into the First Division. Appalling home form — which included home defeat against fellow strugglers Bradford City — as well as defeat by Burnley in the FA Cup saw Derby play more like lambs than rams. Fortunately, the season gradually came good and the team secured its Premier League place for 2000/01 with a home draw against Newcastle United in the penultimate game of the season. With a squad strengthened by the signing of Georgi Kinkladzi and by the emergence of new talent such as Malcolm Christie, the Bald Eagle's team will be expected to perform much better in the new season.

EVERTON

Goodison Park, Goodison Road, Liverpool, L4 4EL

Tel No: 0151 330 2200
Advance Tickets Tel No: 0151 330 2300
Fax: 0151 286 9112
Web Site: www.evertonfc.com
E-Mail: everton@evertonfc.com
League: F.A. Premier
Brief History: Founded 1879 as St. Domingo, changed to Everton in 1880. Former grounds: Stanley Park, Priory Road and Anfield (Liverpool F.C. Ground), moved to Goodison Park in 1892. Founder-members Football League (1888). Record attendance 78,299
(Total) Current Capacity: 40,260 all seated
Visiting Supporters' Allocation: 2,726
Club Colours: Blue and white shirts, white shorts
Nearest Railway Station: Liverpool Lime Street

Parking (Car): Corner of Utting and Priory Avenues
Parking (Coach/Bus): Priory Road
Police Force and Tel No: Merseyside (0151 709 6010)
Disabled Visitors' Facilities:
  Wheelchairs: Bullens Road Stand
  Blind: Commentary available
Anticipated Development(s): Following a period when it looked as though the club had reversed its previous policy of relocating in favour of redevelopment at Goodison, it now looks as though the new consortium led by Bill Kenwright is investigating the possibility of relocation again given the constraints upon expansion at Goodison.

KEY

C Club Offices
S Club Shop
E Entrance(s) for visiting supporters
R Refreshment bars for visiting supporters
T Toilets for visiting supporters

↑ North direction (approx)

❶ A580 Walton Road
❷ Bullen Road
❸ Goodison Road
❹ Car Park
❺ Liverpool Lime Street BR Station (2 miles)
❻ To M57 Junction 2, 4 and 5
❼ Stanley Park

ith ownership of the club now resolved and with the unpopular chairman Peter Johnson now a figure
the past, Everton fans had more to cheer both on and off the field in 1999/2000 than for a number of
asons. In the past few years, the Toffees have flirted with relegation. In 1998/99 it was the prowess of
a loan Kevin Campbell in front of goal that helped to keep the team in the Premier League; in
999/2000, aided by impressive form at Goodison — where the team only lost three times all season —
e club was never in any serious danger of anything worse than a position of mid-table mediocrity.
owever, with Liverpool apparently resurgent, the blue half of Merseyside will be hoping for a vast
nprovement in 2000/01 from a team traditionally considered to be one of the 'Big Five' of English
otball.

EXETER CITY

St. James Park, Exeter, EX4 6PX

Tel No: 01392 254073
Advance Tickets Tel No: 01392 254073
Fax: 01392 425885
Web Site: www.ecfc.demon.co.uk
League: 3rd Division
Brief History: Founded in 1904. (From amalgamation of St. Sidwell United and Exeter United.) Founder-members Third Division (1920). Record attendance 20,984
(Total) Current Capacity: 10,000 (5,100 seated)
Visiting Supporters' Allocation: 1,274
Club Colours: Red and white striped shirts, white shorts
Nearest Railway Station: Exeter St. James Park
Parking (Car): National Car Park and Council Car Parks (No street parking)
Parking (Coach/Bus): Paris Street bus station
Police Force and Tel No: Devon and Cornwall (01392 52101)

Disabled Visitors' Facilities:
Wheelchairs: St James Road entrance (prior booking
Blind: No special facility
Anticipated Development(s): Following a period when the club's survival was seriously in doubt, work commenced during the 1999/2000 season on the reconstruction of St James Park. The first section of the ground to be reconstructed was the Big Bank Terrace — opened in March 2000 — that now provides covered accommodation over the rebuilt terrace. The old Cow Shed was closed during the season and demolished with a new stand under construction. This new 2,200-seat stand is scheduled for completion for the start of the 2000/01 season. Beyond this, the club proposes a minor realignment of the pitch to allow redevelopment of the St James Road End in due course.

KEY

C Club Offices

E Entrance(s) for visiting supporters

R Refreshment bars for visiting supporters

T Toilets for visiting supporters

↑ North direction (approx)

❶ Exeter St. James Park BR Station
❷ St. James Road
❸ Old Tiverton Road
❹ Blackboy Road
❺ Well Street

Above: 684547; *Right:* 684544

68

Dispensing with Peter Fox during the course of the season, the Grecians, despite stirring FA Cup performances against Everton, the club appointed Noel Blake as his replacement. The new appointment was, however, unable to prevent the team's gradual drift down the Third Division table. Enough points were gathered during the course of the season to ensure that the team was never dragged down into the relegation battle, but finishing 21st bodes ill for the future, particularly given the team's defeat on the last day to then bottom team Shrewsbury Town, thereby allowing the Shrews to avoid the drop.

OLD TIVERTON ROAD

COWSHED
UNDER REDEVELOPMENT

PITCH SIZE
113 X 71 yards

BIG BANK
COVERED TERRACE

St JAMES ROAD END
UNCOVERED TERRACE
AWAY

St JAMES ROAD

DISABLED FANS

MAIN GRANDSTAND

AWAY

FULHAM

Craven Cottage, Stevenage Road, Fulham, London, SW6 6HH

Tel No: 020 7893 8383
Advance Tickets Tel No: 020 7384 4710
Fax: 020 7384 4715
Web Site: www.fulhamfc.co.uk
League: 1st Division
Brief History: Founded in 1879 as St. Andrews Fulham, changed name to Fulham in 1898. Former Grounds: Star Road, Ranelagh Club, Lillie Road, Eel Brook Common, Purser's Cross, Barn Elms and Half Moon (Wasps Rugby Football Ground), moved to Craven Cottage in 1894. Record attendance 49,335
(Total) Current Capacity: 18,623 (7,023 seated)
Visiting Supporters' Allocation: 4,600 (600 seated) in Riverside Stand and Putney Terrace
Club Colours: White shirts, black shorts
Nearest Railway Station: Putney Bridge (Tube)

Parking (Car): Street parking
Parking (Coach/Bus): Stevenage Road
Police Force and Tel No: Metropolitan (020 7741 6212)
Disabled Visitors' Facilities:
   Wheelchairs: Main Stand and Hammersmith End
   Blind: No special facility
Anticipated Development(s): Although parts of the ground — Craven Cottage and part of the Stevenage Road Stand (recently restored) — are listed, there are plans for the development of a 30,000 all-seater stadium. Following the reseating of the Riverside Stand, work will next be focused on the Putney End, where it is likely that a 4,500-seat stand will be constructed. If this takes place, then away fans will be relocated.

KEY

- **C** Club Offices
- **S** Club Shop
- **E** Entrance(s) for visiting supporters
- **R** Refreshment bars for visiting supporters
- **T** Toilets for visiting supporters

↑ North direction (approx)

- **1** River Thames
- **2** Stevenage Road
- **3** Finlay Street
- **4** Putney Bridge Tube Station (1/2 mile)
- **5** Putney Terrace
- **6** Riverside Stand
- **7** Main Stand
- **8** Hammersmith End
- **9** Craven Cottage

Above: 685839; *Right:* 685834

Although the season started brightly for Paul Bracewell and Fulham and with notable cup successes in both the FA and Worthington cups, failure to achieve either an automatic promotion place or a spot in the Play-Offs was to cost Bracewell his job. With Mohammed Al-Fayed as a highly ambitious chairman and with a strong squad of players — including Karl-Heinz Reidle signed from Liverpool during the season who took over temporarily from Bracewell — the new manager, Frenchman Jean Tigana, will discover quickly that the chairman will take few prisoners in his desire to bring Premier League football to Craven Cottage.

STEVENAGE ROAD

MAIN STAND

THE COTTAGE

HAMMERSMITH END
COVERED TERRACE

UNCOVERED TERRACE
DISABLED FANS

DISABLED FANS

PITCH SIZE
110 X 75 yards

PUTNEY END
UNCOVERED TERRACE
AWAY

BISHOPS PARK

RIVERSIDE STAND

RIVER THAMES

GILLINGHAM

Priestfield Stadium, Redfern Avenue, Gillingham, Kent, ME7 4DD

Tel No: 01634 300000
Advance Tickets Tel No: 01634 851854
Fax: 01634 850986
Web Site: gillinghamfootballclub.com
League: 1st Division
Brief History: Founded 1893, as New Brompton, changed name to Gillingham in 1913. Founder-members Third Division (1920). Lost Football League status (1938), re-elected to Third Division South (1950). Record attendance 23,002
(Total) Current Capacity: 14,325 (10,525 seated)
Visiting Supporters' Allocation: 1,800 (in Redfern Terrace Avenue Corner Terrace)
Club Colours: Blue and Black striped shirts, black shorts
Nearest Railway Station: Gillingham
Parking (Car): Street parking
Parking (Coach/Bus): As directed by Police
Police Force and Tel No: Kent (01634 834488)
Disabled Visitors' Facilities:
Wheelchairs: Redfern Avenue
Blind: No special facility
Anticipated Development(s): Work continues on the redevelopment of Priestfield. The Rainham End Stand has now been completed and work is well in hand on the construction of the new two-tier Main Stand. It has been decided that the new facility will be called the Medway Stand.

KEY

E Entrance(s) for visiting supporters

↑ North direction (approx)

❶ Redfern Avenue
❷ Toronto Road
❸ Gordon Road
❹ Gillingham BR station (1/4 mile)
❺ Gordon Street Stand
❻ New two-tier Main (Medway) Stand (under construction)
❼ New Rainham End Stand
❽ Gillingham End; uncovered terrace

Above: 684560; *Right:* 684552

Following the huge disappointment of the 1998/99 Play-Off final — where the Gills allowed Manchester City to grab a draw (and then win on penalties) when being 2-0 up — and the departure of previous manager Tony Pulis, new boss Peter Taylor was faced by the need to keep the team's spirits and performances up. Claiming two notable Premier League scalps — Bradford City and Sheffield Wednesday — in the FA Cup was a foretaste for another campaign in the Play-Offs as the team finished 1999/2000 in third spot. Last day defeat at Wrexham, combined with Burnley's victory over Scunthorpe resulted in the Lancashire side joining Preston North End automatically in the First Division. Defeated 3-2 at Stoke in the first leg of the Play-Off semi-final, the Gills won the return leg 3-0 to face Wigan in the final at Wembley. Unlike the disappointment of 1999, the Gills' trip to Wembley in 2000 resulted in victory 3-2 after extra time bringing First Division to the club for the first time in its 107-year history.

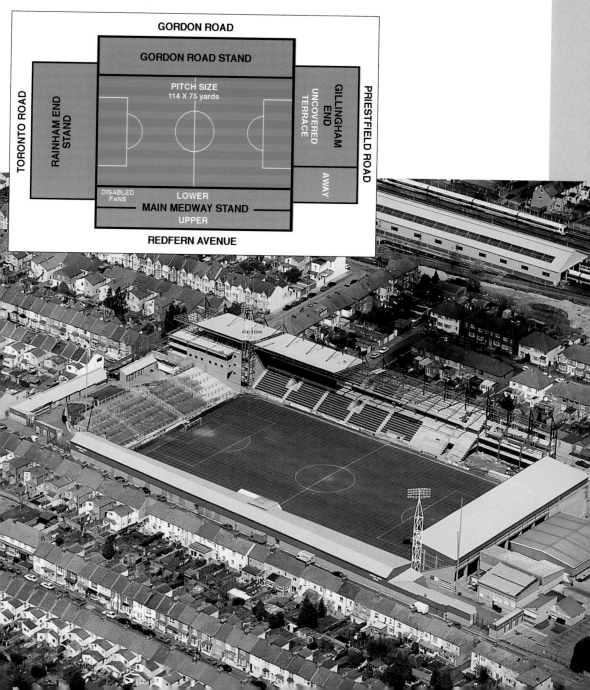

GRIMSBY TOWN

Blundell Park, Cleethorpes, DN35 7PY

Tel No: 01472 605050
Advance Tickets Tel No: 01472 605050
Fax: 01472 693665
Web Site: www.gtfc.co.uk
E-Mail: mariners@gcfc.co.uk
League: 1st Division
Brief History: Founded in 1878, as Grimsby Pelham, changed name to Grimsby Town in 1879. Former Grounds: Clee Park (two adjacent fields) and Abbey Park, moved to Blundell Park in 1899. Founder-members 2nd Division (1892). Record attendance 31,651

(Total) Current Capacity: 10,033 (all seated)
Visiting Supporters' Allocation: 1,874
Club Colours: Black and white striped shirts, black shorts
Nearest Railway Station: Cleethorpes
Parking (Car): Street parking
Parking (Coach/Bus): Harrington Street
Police Force and Tel No: Humberside (01472 359171)
Disabled Visitors' Facilities:
  Wheelchairs: Harrington Street
  Blind: Commentary available

KEY

C Club Offices
S Club Shop
E Entrance(s) for visiting supporters
R Refreshment bars for visiting supporters
T Toilets for visiting supporters

↑ North direction (approx)

❶ A180 Grimsby Road
❷ Cleethorpes BR Station (1½ miles)
❸ To Grimsby and M180 Junction 5
❹ Harrington Street
❺ Constitutional Avenue
❻ Humber Estuary

Following 1998/99, when (the now departed) Alan Buckley's team consolidated its position in the First Division after promotion the season before, 1999/2000 turned out to be something of a disappointment for the Mariners. No doubt the loss of a number of key players as a result of the Bosman ruling during the close season, but an inability to score goals also undermined the team's position. In many respects, 1999/2000 was a move backwards for the team with a position just above the relegation zone being a major setback. Although the team possesses a number of promising youngsters, confidence will be at a low ebb unless goals start to flow early in the new season.

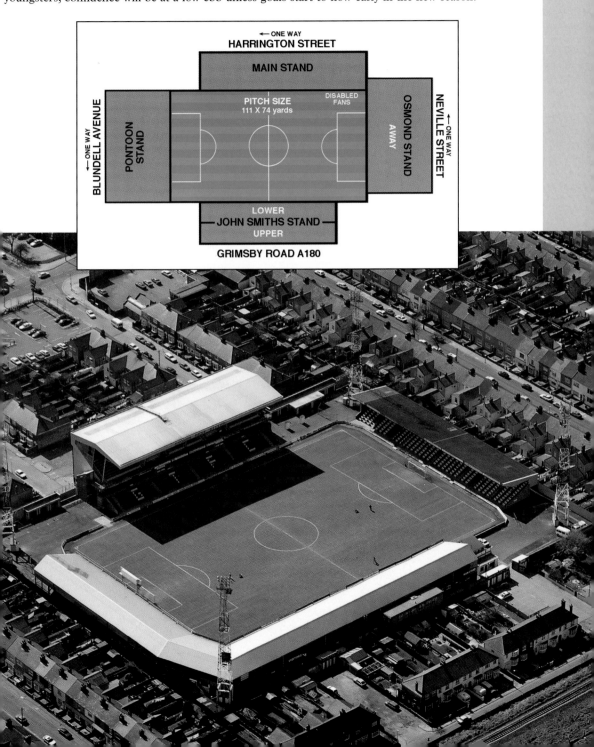

HALIFAX TOWN

Shay Ground, Halifax, West Yorkshire HX1 2YS

Tel No: 01422 353423
Advance Tickets Tel No: 01422 353423
League: 3rd Division
Brief History: Founded 1911; elected to the
Football League in 1921. Relegated from the
Football League to Vauxhall Conference at the
end of the 1992/93 season; won Vauxhall
Conference title and promoted to Third Division
in 1997/98. Record attendance 36,885
(Total) Current Capacity: 9,927 (1,830 seated)
Visiting Supporters' Allocation: 3,800 in North
Stand
Club Colours: Blue and white shirts, blue and
white shorts
Nearest Railway Station: Halifax
Parking (Car): There is a car park at the ground;
access for pass holders only. Also car park at the
corner of Skircoat Road and Hunger Hill. Also
street parking

Parking (Coach/Bus): As directed
Police Force and Tel No: West Yorkshire (01422
3603333)
Disabled Visitors' Facilities:
  Wheelchairs: Approximately 36 places
  Blind: Commentary available
Anticipated Development(s): Work on the
roofing of the South Terrace has been completed
and attention has turned to the North Terrace,
where away fans will be located for the 2000/01
season. The old Main Stand has been demolished
and work is in hand for the construction of a new
facility. The next phase includes the construction
of a new Skircoat Road Stand with the ultimate
aim of achieving a 15,000 capacity at the ground.
Work is being undertaken in conjunction with the
ground's owner (Calderdale MBC) and with the
co-tenants, Halifax Blue Sox RLFC.

KEY

⬆ North direction (approx)

❶ Skircoat Road
❷ Heath Road
❸ Hunger Hill
❹ Bus Depot
❺ To station (0.5 miles)
❻ Shaw Syke
❼ To M62 (Junction 24) via
A629
❽ Shaw Hill
❾ To Town Centre (0.25 miles)
❿ Skircoat Stand
⓫ North Stand
⓬ Main Stand (under
construction)
⓭ South Stand

Above: 685553; Right: 685547

The second season back in the Nationwide League was always going to prove a struggle for the Shaymen, particularly with a new manager — Mark Lillis — in charge and without the prolific Geoff Horsfield — sold to Fulham during the 1998/99 season — up front. Although starting promisingly, the season gradually evolved into a gradual slide down the Third Division table; never bad enough to get sucked into the relegation mire but not good enough to mount a sustained challenge on even a Play-Off spot. Finishing 18th at the end of the season will be regarded as a considerable disappointment and, unless the team's form picks up quickly at the start of the new season, 2000/01 could prove to be a long battle against a return to the Conference.

SKIRCOAT STAND
BEING REBUILT

PITCH SIZE
110 X 76 yards

DISABLED
10 PLACES

SOUTH TERRACE
COVERED TERRACE

NORTH STAND
COVERED TERRACE
AWAY

HANGER HILL

DISABLED
FANS

MAIN STAND

SHAW HILL   SHAY SKYE

HARTLEPOOL UNITED

Victoria Park, Clarence Road, Hartlepool, TS24 8BZ

Tel No: 01429 272584
Advance Tickets Tel No: 01429 272584
Web Site: www.hartlepoolunited.co.uk
E-Mail: info@hartlepoolunited.co.uk
Fax: 01429 863007
League: 3rd Division
Brief History: Founded 1808 as Hartlepools United, changed to Hartlepool (1968) and to Hartlepool United in 1977. Founder-members 3rd Division (1921). Record attendance 17,426
(Total) Current Capacity: 7,229 (3,966 seated)
Visiting Supporters' Allocation: 741 (located in Rink Stand)
Club Colours: Blue and white striped shirts, blue shorts

Nearest Railway Station: Hartlepool Church Street
Parking (Car): Street parking and rear of clock garage
Parking (Coach/Bus): As directed
Police Force and Tel No: Cleveland (01429 221151
Disabled Visitors' Facilities:
  Wheelchairs: Cyril Knowles Stand
  Blind: Commentary available
Anticipated Development(s): The plans for the redevelopment of the Millhouse Stand are still progressing, although there is now no definite timescale. When this work does commence, the ground's capacity will be reduced to 5,000.

KEY

C Club Offices
S Club Shop
E Entrance(s) for visiting supporters

▮ North direction (approx)

❶ A179 Clarence Road
❷ Hartlepool Church Street BR Station
❸ Marina Way
❹ Site of former Greyhound Stadium
❺ To Middlesbrough A689 & A1(M)
❻ To A19 North
❼ Rink Stand

Above: 680637; Right: 680641

In 1998/99 Hartlepool United were one of the teams at the wrong end of the Third Division and many of the pundits expected the team to perform even worse in 1999/2000 with relegation from the Nationwide League being a real possibility. In fact, the team prospered under Chris Turner and, whilst never good enough to threaten automatic promotion, did sneak into the last Play-Off sport courtesy of Cheltenham's defeat at Southend and Hartlepool's win away at Hull. However, rivals Darlington defeated United over the two legs to ensure Third Division football again at Victoria Park in 2000/01.

HUDDERSFIELD TOWN

The Alfred McAlpine Stadium, Leeds Road, Huddersfield, HD1 6PX

Tel No: 01484 484100
Advance Tickets Tel No: 01484 484123
Fax: 01484 484101
Web Site: www.huddersfield-town.co.uk
E-Mail: ht.afc@virgin.net
League: 1st Division
Brief History: Founded 1908, elected to Football League in 1910. First Club to win the Football League Championship three years in succession. Moved from Leeds Road ground to Kirklees (Alfred McAlpine) Stadium 1994/95 season. Record attendance (Leeds Road) 67,037; McAlpine Stadium: 22,129
(Total) Current Capacity: 24,000 (all seated)
Visiting Supporters' Allocation: 4,037 (all seated)

Club Colours: Blue and white striped shirts , white shorts
Nearest Railway Station: Huddersfield
Parking (Car): Car parks adjacent to ground
Parking (Coach/Bus): Car parks adjacent to ground
Police Force and Tel No: West Yorkshire (01484 422122)
Disabled Visitors' Facilities:
  Wheelchairs: Three sides of Ground, at low levels and raised area, including toilet access
  Blind: Area for Partially sighted with Hospital Radio commentary
Anticipated Development(s): With completion of the new North Stand, work on the McAlpine Stadium is over.

KEY

C Club Offices
S Club Shop
E Entrance(s) for visiting supporters

↑ North direction (approx)

❶ To Leeds and M62 Junction 25
❷ A62 Leeds Road
❸ To Huddersfield BR station (1¼ miles)
❹ Disabled parking
❺ Town Avenue pay car park (on site of former ground)
❻ North Stand
❼ St Andrews pay car park
❽ Coach park
❾ South Stand (away)

Above: 679683; Right: 679681

A highly disappointing season for Steve Bruce and Huddersfield Town saw the team topping the table early on and then being in a Play Off place for the rest of the season — until results from the last Sunday of the season. A 1-0 victory for Bolton Wanderers combined with a 3-0 defeat for the Terriers at Fulham meant that the Lancashire team leapfrogged Town into the Play-Offs and consigned ambitious Huddersfield to the First Division for 2000/01. Whilst Town undoubtedly had a talented team, it will be interesting to see if Bruce is able to retain them all. During the season, prolific striker Marcus Stewart was transferred to promotion rivals Ipswich Town despite having signed a new contract earlier in the season. The new season will bring local derbies against the two Sheffield teams and Barnsley, but Terriers' fans would no doubt have preferred the possibility of trying their luck at Leeds and Bradford instead.

HULL CITY

Boothferry Park, Boothferry Road, Hull, HU4 6EU

Tel No: 01482 575263
Advance Tickets Tel No: 01482 575263
Fax: 01482 565752
E-Mail: info@hullcity.org.uk
League: 3rd Division
Brief History: Founded 1904. Former grounds: The Boulevard (Hull Rugby League Ground), Dairycoates, Anlaby Road Cricket Circle (Hull Cricket Ground), Anlaby Road, moved to Boothferry Park in 1946. Record attendance 55,019
(Total) Current Capacity: 15,160 (5,262 seated)
Visiting Supporters' Allocation: 1,859 (535 seated)
Club Colours: Amber with black and white trim shirts, black shorts

Nearest Railway Station: Hull Paragon
Parking (Car): Street Parking and at ground (limited)
Parking (Coach/Bus): At ground
Police Force and Tel No: Humberside (01482 220148)
Disabled Visitors' Facilities:
  Wheelchairs: Corner East/South stands
  Blind: Commentary available
Anticipated Development(s): With the ground's ownership still unresolved, future plans remain subject to confirmation. It has been suggested that a new (4,500 capacity) stand may be built on the east side, but this is dependent on funding. There is unlikely to be any significant development for the next 12 months.

KEY

C Club Offices
S Club Shop
E Entrance(s) for visiting supporters

↑ North direction (approx)

❶ A63 Boothferry Road
❷ North Road
❸ Hull Paragon BR Station (1¹/₂ miles)
❹ To Humber Bridge and M62 Junction 38

Above: 612976; Right: 612986

A position of mid-table safety was probably as much as long-suffering fans of City could expect after the previous season when the team flirted with relegation to the Conference. However, the club's position remains tenuous. Although departing from the scene during the 1998/99 season, previous chairman David Lloyd still owns Boothferry Park and, in late May, the club's staff were locked out as a result of, it was reported, non-payment of rent. Given that the club's current board is also riven by dissent, prospects for football on Humberside don't look too bright. On the assumption that the (toothless) Tigers have somewhere to play their home games in 2000/01, fans can expect another season of strife.

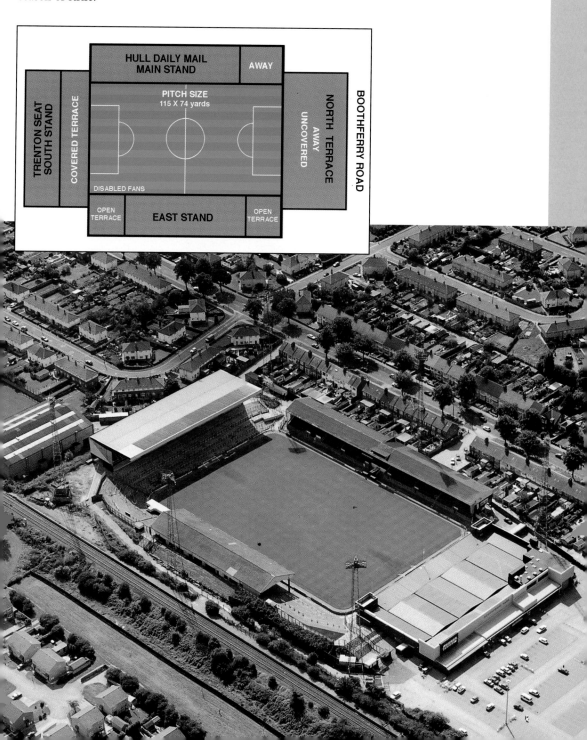

HULL DAILY MAIL MAIN STAND

AWAY

PITCH SIZE
115 X 74 yards

TRENTON SEAT SOUTH STAND

COVERED TERRACE

NORTH TERRACE
AWAY UNCOVERED

BOOTHFERRY ROAD

DISABLED FANS

OPEN TERRACE

EAST STAND

OPEN TERRACE

IPSWICH TOWN

Portman Road, Ipswich, IP1 2DA

Tel No: 01473 400500
Advance Tickets Tel No: 0845 6050129
Fax: 01473 400040
Web Site: http://www.itfc.co.uk
E-Mail: enquiries@itfc.co.uk
League: FA Premier League
Brief History: Founded 1887 as Ipswich Association F.C., changed to Ipswich Town in 1888. Former Grounds: Broom Hill & Brookes Hall, moved to Portman Road in 1888. Record attendance 38,010
(Total) Current Capacity: 22,600 all seated
Visiting Supporters' Allocation: 1,771 all seated in Cobbold Stand

Club Colours: Blue shirts, white shorts
Nearest Railway Station: Ipswich
Parking (Car): Portman Road, Portman Walk & West End Road
Parking (Coach/Bus): West End Road
Police Force and Tel No: Suffolk (01473 611611)
Disabled Visitors' Facilities:
  Wheelchairs: Lower Pioneer Stand
  Blind: Commentary available
Anticipated Development(s): Nothing anticipated

KEY

C Club Offices

S Club Shop

E Entrance(s) for visiting supporters

R Refreshment bars for visiting supporters

T Toilets for visiting supporters

⬆ North direction (approx)

❶ A137 West End Road
❷ Portman Walk
❸ Portman Road
❹ Princes Street
❺ Ipswich BR Station
❻ Car Parks

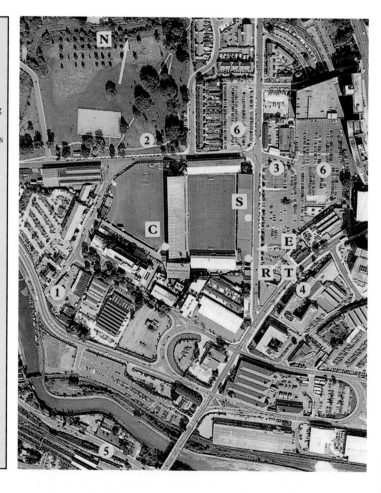

Another season, another third place, another encounter with the Play-Offs. How much all those associated with Ipswich must hate the system. Again pipped for automatic promotion — this time by Manchester City — George Burley's team once more faced the prospect of the Play-Offs. In the past three seasons Ipswich have been defeated at this stage. However, victory over Bolton Wanderers — gaining sweet revenge for defeat at the same stage last season — saw Town return to Wembley and a final showdown with Barnsley, conquerors of Birmingham City. Despite going 1-0 down, Town eventually emerged victorious 4-2 thus restoring top flight football to East Anglia.

KIDDERMINSTER HARRIERS

Aggborough Stadium, Hoo Road, Kidderminster, Worcestershire DY10 1NB

Tel No: 01562 823931
Advance Tickets Tel No: 01562 823931
Fax: 01562 827329
Web Site: http://www.harriers.co.uk
E-Mail: info@harriers.co.uk
League: 3rd Division
Brief History: The club was established in 1886. There have been no previous grounds. The team won the Nationwide Conference title at the end of the 1999/2000 season and entered the Nationwide League for 2000/01 season. Record attendance at Aggborough Stadium: 9,155
(Total) Current Capacity: 6,237 (1,107 seated)
Visiting Supporters' Allocation: 1,300 (all unseated in South [College End] Terrace)

Club Colours: Red shirts with white markings; red shorts
Nearest Railway Station: Kidderminster
Parking (Car): Limited at ground parking otherwise on-street
Parking (Coach/Bus): As directed
Police Force and Tel No: West Mercia (01562 820888
Disabled Visitors' Facilities:
Wheelchairs: Designated section in front of George Reynolds Stand
Blind: No special facility
Anticipated Development(s): The club is looking either to redevelop the existing ground or to relocate. Nothing, however, is as yet finalised.

KEY

C Club Offices
S Club Shop
E Entrance(s) for visiting supporters

↑ North direction (approx)

❶ South (College) End – away
❷ Kidderminster Town station (Severn Valley Railway)
❸ Kidderminster station
❹ Hoo Road
❺ Constitution Hill Ringway
❻ To Town Centre (half a mile)
❼ Chester Road South
❽ To A449 and M5 (14 miles)
❾ Stadium Close
❿ Car park
⓫ Harriers Trading Estate
⓬ Vicarage Close

Above: 685564; Right: 685558

Cruelly denied automatic promotion some years ago when the club's ground was deemed unsuitable for League football, few will begrudge Kidderminster Harriers their success in bringing Nationwide League football to Worcestershire. Now managed by Jan Molby, the former Liverpool and Denmark player and erstwhile manager at Swansea, the club's success means that the big non-league spenders — Rushden & Diamonds — again failed to capitalise upon their wealth and remain in the Conference. In recent years, the clubs that have achieved automatic promotion from the Conference have prospered in the Nationwide League and fans will be expecting Harriers to threaten a Play-Off place at the very least.

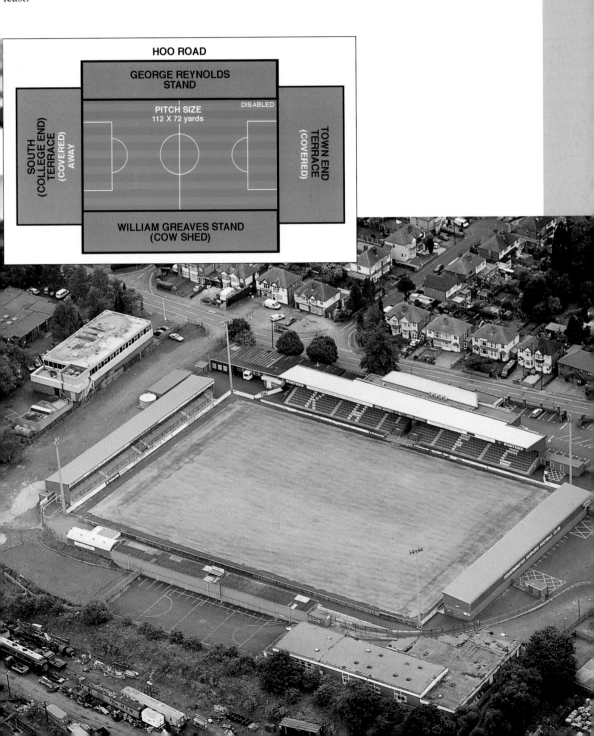

LEEDS UNITED

Elland Road, Leeds, LS11 0ES

Tel No: 0113 226 6000
Advance Tickets Tel No: 0113 226 1000
Fax: 0113 226 6050
Web Site: www.lufc.co.uk
League: F.A. Premier
Brief History: Founded 1919, formed from the former 'Leeds City' Club, who were disbanded following expulsion from the Football League in October 1919. Joined Football League in 1920. Record attendance 57,892
(Total) Current Capacity: 40,294 (all seated)
Visiting Supporters' Allocation: 1,725 in South East Corner (can be increased to 3,662 in South Stand if necessary)
Club Colours: White shirts, white shorts
Nearest Railway Station: Leeds City
Parking (Car): Car parks adjacent to ground
Parking (Coach/Bus): As directed by Police
Police Force and Tel No: West Yorkshire (0113 243 5353)
Disabled Visitors' Facilities:
   Wheelchairs: West Stand and South Stand
   Blind: Commentary available
Anticipated Development(s): Nothing anticipated.

KEY

C Club Offices
S Club Shop
E Entrance(s) for visiting supporters

↑ North direction (approx)

❶ M621
❷ M621 Junction 2
❸ A643 Elland Road
❹ Lowfields Road
❺ To A58
❻ City Centre and BR station
❼ To M62 and M1

In David O'Leary's first full season in charge, Leeds United proved themselves — on their day — to be one of the most attractive footballing teams in the Premier League. With an abundance of youthful talent — in particular figures like Harry Kewell — United were at the top of the table early on before the awesome power of Manchester United overwhelmed them and the rest of the Premier League. Relative success at home was matched by a promising campaign in Europe; however, the latter was marred by ugly scenes in Turkey during the away leg of the UEFA Cup semi-final which resulted in the death of two Leeds' fans. Failure to turn around the 2-0 deficit in the home game mean that Leeds' interest in Europe ended in 1999/2000, but having pipped Liverpool for the third spot in the Premier League means that United now have the opportunity of playing for a place in the Champions' League in 2000/01. With the squad being strengthened with several acquisitions in the close season, such as Olivier Dacourt from Lens, means that United will be better placed to mount a strong challenge both domestically and in Europe in the new season.

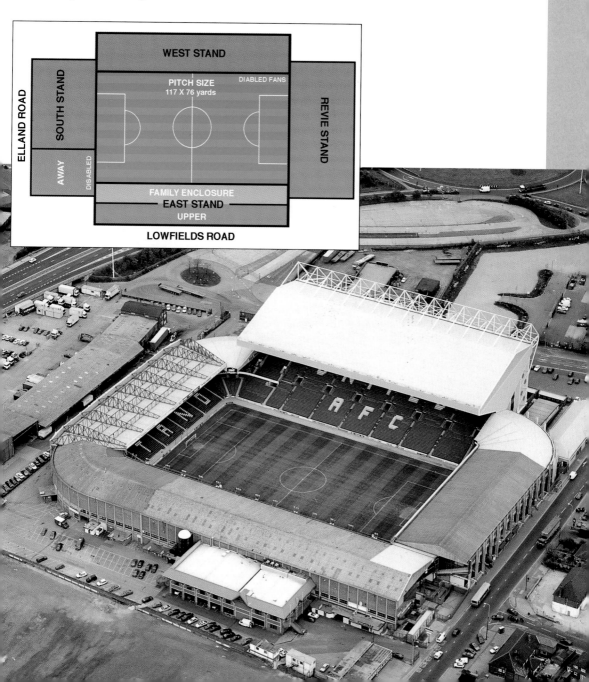

LEICESTER CITY

City Stadium, Filbert Street, Leicester, LE2 7FL

Tel No: 0116 291 5000
Advance Tickets Tel No: 0116 291 5296
Fax: 0116 291 1249
Web Site: www.lcfc.co.uk
League: F.A. Premier
Brief History: Founded 1884 as Leicester Fosse, changed name to Leicester City in 1919. Former Grounds: Fosse Road South, Victoria Road, Belgrave Cycle Track, Mill Lane and Aylestone Road Cricket Ground, moved to Filbert Street in 1891. Record attendance 47,298
(Total) Current Capacity: 21,500 (all seated)
Visiting Supporters' Allocation: 2,011 in East Stand Blocks T and U
Club Colours: Blue shirts, white shorts

Nearest Railway Station: Leicester
Parking (Car): NCP car park and street parking
Parking (Coach/Bus): Western Boulevard
Police Force and Tel No: Leicester (0116 253 0066)
Disabled Visitors' Facilities:
  Wheelchairs: 67 places in Carling, South and East Stands
  Blind: Commentary available
Anticipated Development(s): Although plans for the construction of a new stadium at Bede Island were approved in 1999, the package for the construction of the new ground failed to materialise, with the result that City were left without any option other than, at the current time, to redevelop at Filbert Street.

KEY

C Club Offices
S Club Shop
E Entrance(s) for visiting supporters
R Refreshment bars for visiting supporters
T Toilets for visiting supporters

↑ North direction (approx)

❶ Walnut Street
❷ Filbert Street
❸ Grasmere Street
❹ River Soar
❺ M1 and M69 Junction 21
❻ Leicester BR Station (1 mile)

Whilst weakened through transfer and injury, with Emile Heskey being transferred to Liverpool and recent signing Stan Collymore breaking his leg, Martin O'Neill's team reached its highest ever position in the Premier League, finishing in eighth place with a run in of three wins in five games. The season's gloss was, however, was reduced by a last day thrashing at already relegated Sheffield Wednesday, with the Owls coming out on top 4-0. However, success in the Worthington Cup Final means that the season brought silverware to the Filbert Street trophy cabinet and, with it, the prospect of European football in 2000/01. For fans, the major concern must be that, with the collapse of the scheme for the new stadium at Bede Island, Filbert Street remains one of the smallest grounds in the Premier League, giving the club a handicap in capacity terms in relation to other Premier teams. This will be compounded in 2000/01 by the decision of the inspirational O'Neill to jump ship and head north to take over at Celtic.

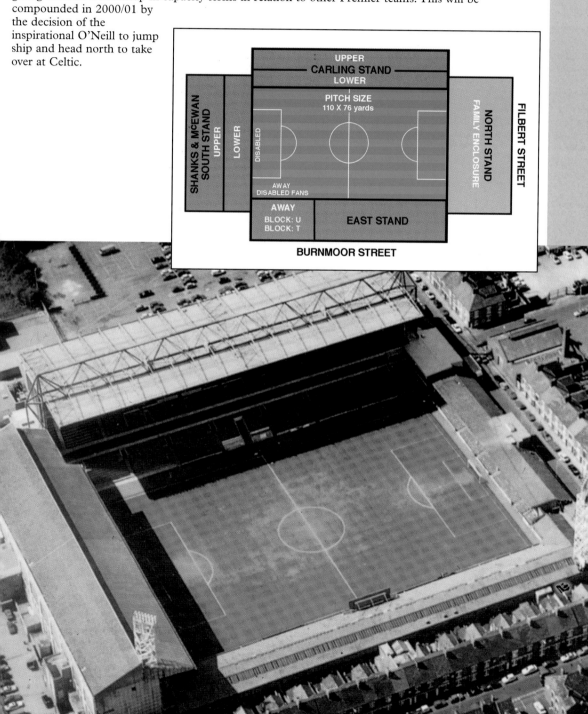

LEYTON ORIENT

Matchroom Stadium, Brisbane Road, Leyton, London, E10 5NF

Tel No: 020 8926 1111
Advance Tickets Tel No: 020 8926 1111
Fax: 020 8539 4390
Web Site: http://leytonorient.com
E-Mail: orient@bigfoot.com
League: 3rd Division
Brief History: Founded 1887 as Clapton Orient, from Eagle Cricket Club (formerly Glyn Cricket Club formed in 1881). Changed name to Leyton Orient (1946), Orient (1966), Leyton Orient (1987). Former grounds: Glyn Road, Whittles Athletic Ground, Millfields Road, Lea Bridge Road, Wembley Stadium (2 games), moved to Brisbane Road in 1937. Record attendance 34,345
(Total) Current Capacity: 13,677 (9,387 seated)
Visiting Supporters' Allocation: 2,154 (932 seated) in East Stand/Terrace

Club Colours: Red shirts, red shorts
Nearest Railway Station: Leyton (tube), Leyton Midland Road
Parking (Car): Street parking
Parking (Coach/Bus): As directed by Police
Police Force and Tel No: Metropolitan (020 8556 8855)
Disabled Visitors' Facilities:
  Wheelchairs: Windsor Road
  Blind: Match commentary supplied on request
Anticipated Development(s): The construction of the much reduced South Stand has now been completed. There remain long term plans for the redevelopment of the other three sides of the ground but, as yet, there is no confirmed schedule for further work.

KEY

C Club Offices
S Club Shop
E Entrance(s) for visiting supporters

↑ North direction (approx)

❶ Buckingham Road
❷ Oliver Road
❸ A112 High Road Leyton
❹ Leyton Tube Station (1/4 mile)
❺ Brisbane Road
❻ Windsor Road
❼ Leyton Midland Road BR station
❽ South Stand

Above: 685578; *Right:* 685572

Widely tipped for automatic promotion or at least a Play-Off berth, an appalling start to the season saw Orient threatened by the very real prospect of relegation to the Nationwide Conference. However, the second half of the season saw the team start to put together some decent results with the result that Tommy Taylor's side finished in 19th place. Given that at the end of 1998/99 the team finished sixth (and in the Play-Offs), such a lowly position can be regarded as a disaster for a team with ambition. Only time will tell as to whether the team reverts to 1998/99 form or again struggles, but the club certainly has the potential to be a force in the Third Division and, in Barry Hearne, a chairman with the track record to achieve it.

LINCOLN CITY

Sincil Bank, Lincoln, LN5 8LD

Tel No: 01522 880011
Advance Tickets Tel No: 01522 880011
Fax: 01522 880020
Web Site: www.redimps.com
E-Mail: lcfc@redimps.com
League: 3rd Division
Brief History: Founded 1884. Former Ground: John O'Gaunts Ground, moved to Sincil Bank in 1895. Founder-members 2nd Division Football League (1892). Relegated from 4th Division in 1987, promoted from GM Vauxhall Conference in 1988. Record attendance 23,196
(Total) Current Capacity: 10,060 (all seated)
Visiting Supporters' Allocation: 1,934 in Stacey West Stand (now all seated)
Club Colours: Red and white striped shirts, black shorts

Nearest Railway Station: Lincoln Central
Parking (Car): City centre car parks; limited on-street parking
Parking (Coach/Bus): South Common
Police Force and Tel No: Lincolnshire (01522 529911)
Disabled Visitors' Facilities:
 Wheelchairs: The Simons and South (Mundy) Park stands
 Blind: No special facility
Anticipated Development(s): Following the replacement of the seats in the Stacey West Stand, Sincil Bank is once again an all-seater stadium. Although there are no immediate plans for further development, the club intends to secure its long term interest in the ground by the acquisition of its freehold.

KEY
C Club Offices
S Club Shop

↑ North direction (approx)

❶ A46 High Street
❷ Sincil Bank
❸ Sausthorpe Street
❹ Cross Street
❺ Linpave Stand
❻ A158 South Park Avenue
❼ Stacey West Stand (away)
❽ Lincoln Central BR Station (½ mile)
❾ Family Stand

Above: 684973; *Right:* 684974

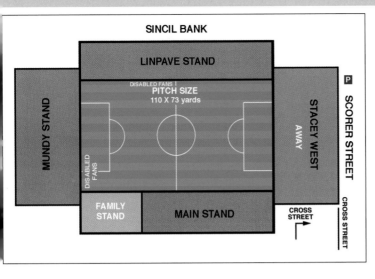

SINCIL BANK

LINPAVE STAND

DISABLED FANS
PITCH SIZE
110 X 73 yards

MUNDY STAND

DISABLED FANS

STACEY WEST
AWAY

P SCORER STREET

CROSS STREET

FAMILY STAND

MAIN STAND

CROSS STREET

Having sacked several managers during his tenure as chairman of the board and having seen the team relegated at the end of the 1998/99 season, John Reames spent the season in charge of the Imps having taken over as manager during the course of 98/99 campaign. At the end of the season it was announced that he was standing down as manager; fans will be expecting his successor, Phil Stamp, to improve significantly on the 15th spot achieved in 1999/2000.

LIVERPOOL

Anfield Road, Liverpool, L4 0TH

Tel No: 0151 263 2361
Advance Tickets Tel No: 0151 260 8680/
  0151 260 9999
Ticket Enquiries Fax: 0151 261 1416
Web Site: http:\\www.liverpoolfc.net
Fax: 0151 260 8813
League: F.A. Premier
Brief History: Founded 1892. Anfield Ground
  formerly Everton F.C. Ground. Joined Football
  League in 1893. Record attendance 61,905
(Total) Current Capacity: 45,362 (all seated)
Visiting Supporters' Allocation: 1,972 (all
  seated) in Anfield Road End
Club Colours: Red shirts, red shorts
Nearest Railway Station: Kirkdale
Parking (Car): Stanley car park
Parking (Coach/Bus): Priory Road and
  Pinehurst Avenue

Police Force and Tel No: Merseyside (0151
  709 6010)
Disabled Visitors' Facilities:
  Wheelchairs: Kop and Main Stands
  Blind: Commentary available
Anticipated Development(s): After examining
  the possibility of expanding Anfield, the club
  has decided to explore the possibility of
  building a new 70,000 stadium costing £150
  million on land about 200yd from Anfield
  adjacent to Stanley Park. If the project
  proceeds, after consultation with the council
  and local residents, it is hoped that the new
  ground will be open for the start of the
  2003/04 season.

KEY

C Club Offices
S Club Shop

⬆ North direction (approx)

❶ Car Park
❷ Anfield Road
❸ A5089 Walton Breck Road
❹ Kemlyn Road
❺ Kirkdale BR Station (1 mile)
❻ Utting Avenue
❼ Stanley Park
❽ Spion Kop
❾ Anfield Road Stand

Under the management of Gerard Houllier, Liverpool proved themselves to be something of a Jekyll and Hyde team in 1999/2000. There were periods when the team seemed to have found the form to make them, once again, a force to be reckoned with, but several tame and ineffective performances towards the end of the season — most notably the home draw against Southampton and the defeat at relegation threatened Bradford City — again cast doubts on the team's true calibre. For much of the second half of the season, Liverpool seemed a certainty to fill one of the Champions' League positions; in the event a failure to score in the final games of the season meant that the Reds will have to be satisfied with the UEFA Cup in 2000/01. With Manchester United continuing to dominate the domestic game, it will be interesting to see how much longer Houllier will be given to create a championship winning team on Merseyside.

LUTON TOWN

Kenilworth Road Stadium, 1 Maple Road, Luton, LU4 8AW

Tel No: 01582 411622
Advance Tickets Tel No: 01582 416976
Fax: 01582 405070
League: 2nd Division
Brief History: Founded 1885 from an amalgamation of Wanderers F.C. and Excelsior F.C. Former Grounds: Dallow Lane & Dunstable Road, moved to Kenilworth Road in 1905. Record attendance 30,069
(Total) Current Capacity: 9,970 (all seated)
Visiting Supporters' Allocation: 2,200
Club Colours: Orange and blue shirts, blue shorts
Nearest Railway Station: Luton
Parking (Car): Street parking
Parking (Coach/Bus): Luton bus station
Police Force and Tel No: Bedfordshire (01582 401212)
Disabled Visitors' Facilities:
  Wheelchairs: Kenilworth Road

Blind: Commentary available
Anticipated Development(s): Like a number of other teams, Luton passed into administration during 1998/99. With the probable demise of the proposed new stadium, attention has been refocused on Kenilworth Road. However, the local authority will not sanction work on the ground that will dwarf existing residential properties and this inevitably restricts what the club can achieve at the existing ground. There are a number of groups keen to take over, but it is uncertain what these consortia plan in terms of ground redevelopment. Following the period of uncertainty, the club was acquired by a new consortium led by Mike Watson-Challis during the close season. As to any future development at Kenilworth Road, nothing has yet been reported.

KEY

- **C** Club Offices
- **S** Club Shop
- **E** Entrance(s) for visiting supporters
- **R** Refreshment bars for visiting supporters
- **T** Toilets for visiting supporters

↑ North direction (approx)

- **❶** To M1 Junction 11
- **❷** Wimborne Road
- **❸** Kenilworth Road
- **❹** Oak Road
- **❺** Dunstable Road
- **❻** Luton BR Station (1 mile)
- **❼** Ticket Office

One of a number of clubs in financial trouble at the start of the season, the club's immediate future was secured at the end of the 1999/2000 by the announcement that it had been bought by Mike Watson-Challis, a former director of the club. Away from financial matters, the Hatters achieved a position of mid-table safety — an improvement over the previous year's dire result but well short of fans' expectations of the team. One of the first actions of the new consortium was to dispense with the services of the increasingly unpopular Lennie Lawrence as manager.

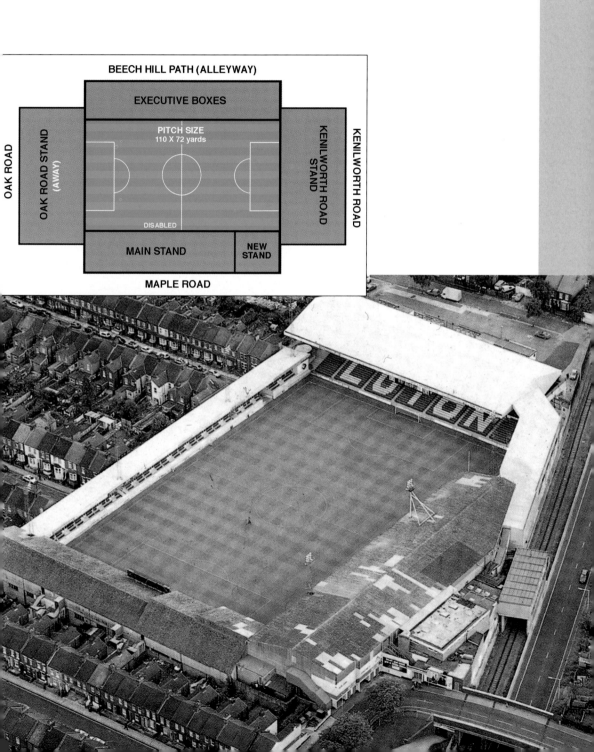

BEECH HILL PATH (ALLEYWAY)

EXECUTIVE BOXES

PITCH SIZE
110 X 72 yards

OAK ROAD

OAK ROAD STAND
(AWAY)

KENILWORTH ROAD
STAND

KENILWORTH ROAD

DISABLED

MAIN STAND

NEW
STAND

MAPLE ROAD

MACCLESFIELD TOWN

Moss Rose Ground, London Road, Macclesfield, SK11 7SP

Tel No: 01625 264686
Advance Tickets Tel No: 01625 264686
Fax: 01625 264692
Web Site: http://www.mtfc.co.uk/
E-Mail: office@mtfc.co.uk
League: 3rd Division
Brief History: Founded 1874. Previous ground: Rostron Field moved to Moss Rose Ground in 1891. Winners of the Vauxhall Conference in 1994/95 and 1997/97. Admitted to Football League for 1997/98 season. Record attendance 9,003
(Total) Current Capacity: 6,307 (2,561 seated)
Visiting Supporters' Allocation: 2,127 (1,500 in Silkman Terrace; 627 seated in Estate Road Stand)
Club Colours: Royal blue, royal blue shorts
Nearest Railway Station: Macclesfield

Parking (Car): No parking at the ground and the nearest off-street car park is in the town centre (25min walk). There is some on-street parking in the vicinity, but this can get crowded.
Parking (Coach/Bus): As directed
Police Force and Tel No: Cheshire (01625 610000)
Disabled Visitors' Facilities:
  Wheelchairs: Limited facilities
  Blind: No special facility
Anticipated Development(s): Although originally it was planned that the next phase of any redevelopment would affect the Silkman Terrace, this is not the case and during 2000/01 the Estate Road Stand will be redeveloped. This may have some consequences for capacity during the season but this cannot be confirmed at the time of going to press.

KEY

C Club Offices
E Entrance(s) for visiting supporters

↑ North direction (approx)

❶ A523 London Road
❷ To Town Centre and BR station (1.5 miles)
❸ To Leek
❹ Moss Lane
❺ Star Lane
❻ Silkmans Public House (now closed)
❼ Star Lane End
❽ Silkman End (away section)
❾ Estate Road Terrace

Following relegation back to the Third Division at the end of the 1998/99 season, 1999/2000 was always going to be one of transition for the Silkmen, particularly after Sammy McIlroy jumped ship to become the new manager of Northern Ireland. For some six years McIlroy had been the team's guiding light as the club moved from the Conference to the Nationwide League and then to the Second Division after only one season in the Third. Despite the loss of the manager and his replacement by Peter Davenport, a position of mid-table anonymity was secured, although fans will be expecting the team to threaten for a Play-Off spot in 2000/01 at the very worst.

MANCHESTER CITY

Maine Road, Moss Side, Manchester, M14 7WN

Tel No: 0161 232 3000
Advance Tickets Tel No: 0161 226 2224
Fax: 0161 232 8999
E-Mail: mcfc@mcfc.co.uk
Web Site: http://www.mcfc.co.uk
League: F.A. Premiership
Brief History: Founded 1880 as West Gorton, changed name to Ardwick (reformed 1887) and to Manchester City in 1894. Former grounds: Clowes Street, Kirkmanshulme Cricket Club, Donkey Common, Pink Bank Lane & Hyde Road, moved to Maine Road in 1923. Founder-members 2nd Division (1892). Record attendance 84,569 (record for Football League ground)
(Total) Current Capacity: 32,147 (all seated)
Visiting Supporters' Allocation: 3,200
Club Colours: Sky blue shirts, white shorts

Nearest Railway Station: Manchester Piccadilly (2½ miles)
Parking (Car): Street parking and local schools
Parking (Coach/Bus): Kippax Street car park
Police Force and Tel No: Greater Manchester (0161 872 5050)
Disabled Visitors' Facilities:
Wheelchairs: Platt Lane Stand/Kippax Stand
Blind: Main Stand 'G' Block
Anticipated Development(s): The plans for the club to move into the new Millennium Stadium, after the completion of the Commonwealth Games of 2002, are progressing. The current intention is that the club will move to the new stadium, with its planned 50,000 capacity, for the start of the 2003/04 season.

KEY

C Club Offices
S Club Shop
E Entrance(s) for visiting supporters

↑ North direction (approx)

❶ Thornton Road
❷ South Upper Lloyd Street
❸ To A5103 Princess Road
❹ To City Centre and Manchester Piccadilly BR Station (2½ miles)
❺ To A6010 & M31 Junction 7
❻ Maine Road
❼ Kippax Stand
❽ Main Stand
❾ Platt Lane Stand

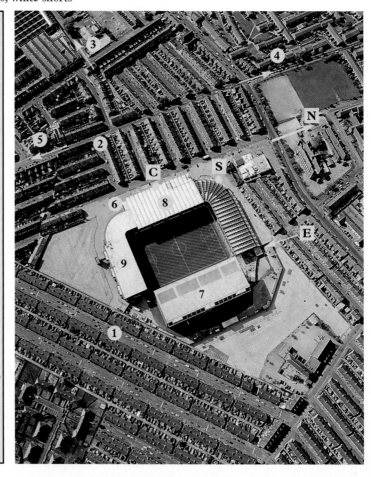

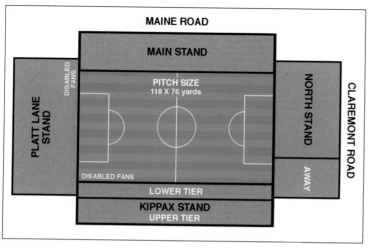

MAINE ROAD

MAIN STAND

PLATT LANE STAND

DISABLED FANS

PITCH SIZE
118 X 76 yards

NORTH STAND

CLAREMONT ROAD

AWAY

DISABLED FANS

LOWER TIER

KIPPAX STAND
UPPER TIER

It's been a dramatic year for Joe Royle's Manchester City. Success at the Second Division Play-Off final against Gillingham in May 1999 after penalties — despite being two-nil down with only minutes to play — has been followed by automatic promotion by finishing second in the First Division to the Premier League. However, promotion was only secured on the final day as a result of a somewhat fortuitous win over Blackburn Rovers. Whilst the new season will bring renewed clashes against United, it will also be a season of considerable struggle if the team is not to follow the usual procession of promoted teams back to the First Division. There will be comparisons made with Watford, who also achieved two promotions to reach the Premier League before being consigned back to the First Division. City no doubt have the potential and fan base to be one of the big teams again, but do they have the squad to prosper in this critical first season?

MANCHESTER UNITED

Old Trafford, Sir Matt Busby Way, Manchester, M16 0RA

Tel No: 0161 868 8000
Advance Tickets Tel No: 0161 868 8020
Fax: 0161 876 5502
Web Site: www.manutd.com
League: F.A. Premier
Brief History: Founded in 1878 as 'Newton Heath L&Y', later Newton Heath, changed to Manchester United in 1902. Former Grounds: North Road, Monsall & Bank Street, Clayton, moved to Old Trafford in 1910 (used Manchester City F.C. Ground 1941-49). Founder-members Second Division (1892). Record attendance 76,962
(Total) Current Capacity: 61,250 (all seated)
Visiting Supporters' Allocation: Approx. 3,000
Club Colours: Red shirts, white shorts
Nearest Railway Station: At Ground
Parking (Car): Lancashire Cricket Ground and White City

Parking (Coach/Bus): As directed by Pollice
Police Force and Tel No: Greater Manchester (0161 872 5050)
Disabled Visitors' Facilities:
  Wheelchairs: South East Stand
  Blind: Commentary available
Anticipated Development(s): Ever onwards and upwards. United completed the second tier of the East (Scoreboard) Stand during 1999/2000 — staging the largest capacity Premiership games in the process — and work is well in hand on the second tier of the West (Stretford End) Stand, taking the capacity to 67,000 during the season. This work will be followed by reconstruction of the South Stand, with the ultimate intention of achieving a capacity of c80,000.

KEY

C Club Offices
S Club Shop

⬆ North direction (approx)

❶ To A5081 Trafford Park Road to M63 Junction 4 (5 miles)
❷ A56 Chester Road
❸ Manchester Ship Canal
❹ To Old Trafford Cricket Ground
❺ To Parking and Warwick Road BR Station
❻ Sir Matt Busby Way

Above: 684990; Right: 684980

After the spectacular triumph of winning the treble at the end of the 1998/99 season, there was always a sense that the new season was going to prove something of an anticlimax for Sir Alex Ferguson's team. In the event, the FA Premier League was retained — the sixth such triumph in eight years — but the club's highly controversial withdrawal from the FA Cup — in order to participate (unsuccessfully) in the FIFA World Club Championship in Brazil — and the failure to beat Spanish opposition in the quarter final of the Champions League meant that the Old Trafford trophy cupboard was uncharacteristically under-utilised. Although, domestically, Man Utd remain the team to beat (and few will bet against them retaining the championship in 2000/01), failure in Europe in 1999/2000 means the team's supposed greatness is suspect. With, no doubt, several high profile signings during the close season, the team should again feature in the latter stages of European competition, but nothing should be taken for granted.

UNITED ROAD

NORTH STAND
TOP TIER
MIDDLE TIER
LOWER TIER

PITCH SIZE
116 X 76 yards

WEST STAND
UPPER
LOWER

EAST STAND
UPPER
LOWER
AWAY

SIR MATT BUSBY WAY

SOUTH STAND

MANSFIELD TOWN

Field Mill Ground, Quarry Lane, Mansfield, Notts, NG18 5DA

Tel No: 01623 623567
Advance Tickets Tel No: 01623 623567
Fax: 01623 625014
League: 3rd Division
Brief History: Founded 1910 as Mansfield Wesleyans Boys Brigade, changed to Mansfield Town in 1914. Former Grounds: Pelham Street, Newgate Lane and The Prairie, moved to Field Mill in 1919. Record attendance 24,467
(Total) Current Capacity: 5,289 (2,695 seated)
Visiting Supporters' Allocation: 1,135 (517 seated) in Bishop Street Stand
Club Colours: Amber with blue trim shirts, Amber shorts with blue trim
Nearest Railway Station: Mansfield
Parking (Car): Car park at Ground

Parking (Coach/Bus): Car park at Ground
Police Force and Tel No: Nottinghamshire (01623 420999)
Disabled Visitors' Facilities:
Wheelchairs: Bishop Street (Entrance at North end of West stand)
Blind: No special facility
Anticipated Development(s): After several years when work was promised, work on the redevelopment of Field Mill finally got underway in 1999/2000. Initially this work involved the demolition of the existing facilities at the North and Quarry Lane ends and their replacement with two 2,200-seat stands. Once completed, attention will turn to the West Stand with the ultimate intention of turning Field Mill into a 10,000 all-seater ground.

KEY

C Club Offices
S Club Shop
E Entrance(s) for visiting supporters
R Refreshment bars for visiting supporters
T Toilets for visiting supporters

↑ North direction (approx)

❶ Car Park
❷ Quarry Lane
❸ A60 Nottingham Road to M1 Junction 27
❹ Portland Street
❺ To A38 and M1 Junction 28
❻ To Town Centre
❼ Mansfield railway station
❽ North End (under construction)
❾ Quarry Lane End (under construction)
❿ Bishop Street Stand (away)
⓫ Main Stand

Above: 685001; Right: 684996

Following the disappointment of 1998/99 when the Stags just missed out on the Play-Offs and manager Steve Parkin resigned — claiming that the position was untenable — new manager Billy Dearden — in his second spell at the club — was faced by the fans' expectations of further progress. In the event, Mansfield struggled and 17th position at the end of 1999/2000 represented a considerable decline. With work now progressing at Field Mill, perhaps a change of scene can bring a change of fortune for the new season. A recommendation of 'don't hold your breath' is perhaps a sensible caveat at this stage, however.

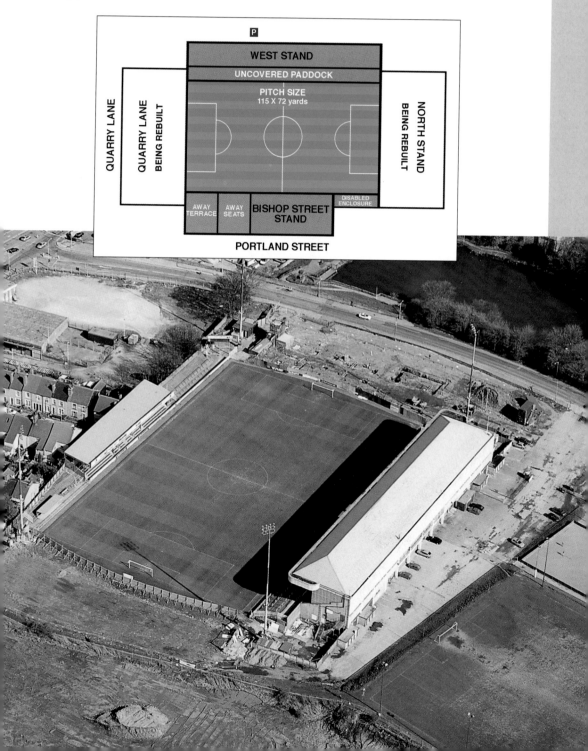

MIDDLESBROUGH

BT Cellnet Riverside Stadium, Middlesbrough, Cleveland

Tel No: 01642 877700
Advance Tickets Tel No: 01642 877745
Fax: 01642 877840
Web Site: www.mfc.co.uk
League: F.A. Premiership
Brief History: Founded 1876. Former Grounds: Archery Ground (Albert Park), Breckon Hill Road, Linthorpe Road, moved to Ayresome Park in 1903, and to current ground in Summer 1995. F.A. Amateur Cup winners 1894 and 1897 (joined Football League in 1899). Record attendance (Ayresome Park) 53,596, (Riverside Stadium) 34,800
(Total) Current Capacity: 35,100 (all seated)
Visiting Supporters' Allocation: 3,450 (in the South Stand)
Club Colours: Red and white shirts, white shorts

Nearest Railway Station: Middlesbrough
Parking (Car): All parking at stadium is for permit holders
Parking (Coach/Bus): As directed
Police Force and Tel No: Cleveland (01642 248184)
Disabled Visitors' Facilities:
 Wheelchairs: More than 360 places available for disabled fans
 Blind: Commentary available
Anticipated Development(s): There remain long term plans for the ground's capacity to be increased to 42,000 through the construction of extra tiers on the North, South and East stands, although there is no confirmed timetable for this work at the current time.

KEY

C Club Offices
S Club Shop

↑ North direction (approx)

❶ Cargo Fleet Road
❷ Middlesbrough station
❸ Middlesbrough town centre
❹ Middlesbrough Docks (1 mile) and Town Centre
❺ A66
❻ Borough Road
❼ Car Park
❽ South Stand

There were times during the season when Bryan Robson's team appeared to be in freefall, heading rapidly towards the dogfight at the Premier League's basement. Despite losing the first game of the season — to promoted Bradford City — the first part of the season indicated that the team might be able to compete for a European place. The second half, however, until the return of on-loan Juninho, was a different story with the team gradually drifting down the table. However, unlike Wimbledon, whose freefall proved terminal, Boro were able to string together enough decent results in the last few weeks of the season to ensure another year of Premier League football at the Riverside. With Juninho's loan period, however, coming to an end along with ageing (and increasingly marginal) stars, it could be another torrid year on Tees-side.

MILLWALL

New Den, Bolina Road, London, SE16 3LN

Tel No: 020 7232 1222
Advance Tickets Tel No: 020 7231 9999
Fax: 020 7231 3663
Web Site: www.millwallfc.co.uk
League: 2nd Division
Brief History: Founded 1885 as Millwall Rovers, changed name to Millwall Athletic (1889) and Millwall (1925). Former Grounds: Glengall Road, East Ferry Road (2 separate Grounds), North Greenwich Ground and The Den – Cold Blow Lane – moved to New Den 1993/94 season. Founder-members Third Division (1920). Record attendance (at The Den) 48,672 (at New Den) 20,093

(Total) Current Capacity: 20,150 (all seated)
Visiting Supporters' Allocation: 4,382
Club Colours: White shirts, silver shorts
Nearest Railway Station: South Bermondsey or Surrey Docks (Tube)
Parking (Car): Juno Way car parking (8 mins walk)
Parking (Coach/Bus): At Ground
Police Force and Tel No: Metropolitan (0171 679 9217)
Disabled Visitors' Facilities:
  Wheelchairs: 200 spaces in West Stand Lower Tier
  Blind: Commentary available

KEY
C Club Offices
S Club Shop
E Entrance(s) for visiting supporters

⬆ North direction (approx)

❶ Bolina Road
❷ South Bermondsey BR
❸ Surrey Quays Underground
❹ Zampa Road
❺ Ilderton Road
❻ To Rotherhithe New Road and Rotherhithe Tunnel
❼ To New Cross
❽ Surrey Canal Road

Having just missed out on the Play-Offs at the end of the 1998/99 season, fans were inevitably expecting some progress in 1999/2000 and, in this, they weren't disappointed. On the fringes of the promotion race throughout, the team, managed by Keith Stevens and Alan McLeary, finished in fifth place, thus earning a Play-Off semi-final against ambitious Wigan Athletic. After two hard fought games — 0-0 at the New Den and 1-0 at the JJB Stadium — it was to be the northern team that battled its way through to Wembley. Provided that the team is able to retain most of its squad, then fans can expect the Lions to be once again threatening for one of the promotion spots in 2000/01.

NEWCASTLE UNITED

St. James' Park, Newcastle-upon-Tyne, NE1 4ST

Tel No: 0191 201 8400
Advance Tickets Tel No: 0191 261 1571
Fax: 0191 201 8600
Web Site: www.nufc.co.uk
League: F.A. Premier
Brief History: Founded in 1882 as Newcastle East End, changed to Newcastle United in 1892. Former Grounds: Chillingham Road, moved to St. James' Park (former home of defunct Newcastle West End) in 1892. Record attendance 68,386
(Total) Current Capacity: 52,000 (all seated)
Visiting Supporters' Allocation: 3,000 in North East Stand
Club Colours: Black and white striped shirts, black shorts
Nearest Railway Station: Newcastle Central

Parking (Car): Leazes car park and street parking
Parking (Coach/Bus): Leazes car park
Police Force and Tel No: Northumbria (0191 232 3451)
Disabled Visitors' Facilities:
  Wheelchairs: 103 spaces available
  Blind: Commentary available
Anticipated Development(s): Work on the construction of the new tiers for the Millburn and Sir John Hall stands is almost complete. This will take the ground's capacity to c52,000. Future redevelopment at St James' Park is problematic, given the lie of the land on the north side, and the club has no immediate plans for further work once the current programme is completed.

KEY

C Club Offices
S Club Shop

↑ North direction (approx)

❶ St. James's Park
❷ Strawberry Place
❸ Gallowgate
❹ Away Section
❺ To Newcastle Central BR Station (¹/₂ mile) & A6127(M)
❻ Car Park
❼ Barrack Road (A189)
❽ To A1 and North
❾ Corporation Street
❿ Percy Road
⓫ Metro Station

Above: 685590; Right: 685581

A disastrous start to the 1999/2000 season, coupled with disagreements with the team's leading players and, worst of all, home defeat against Sunderland, saw manager Ruud Gullit depart from the St James' Park hot seat early in the season. In place of the controversial Dutchman, the powers at Newcastle decided on experience rather than youth and appointed former England boss Bobby Robson – whose age qualified him for a bus pass and, presumably, Senior Citizen concessions at grounds where these are available — to the helm. There was an immediate improvement in both team spirit and performances, which saw the team rapidly lift themselves from the Premier League's basement to a position of some security. There were some disappointments, notably the FA Cup semi-final defeat, but fans of the Magpies can look forward to 2000/01 with some confidence: Alan Shearer continues to score goals and, with Bobby Robson, the club possesses one of the most astute and experienced brains in the game.

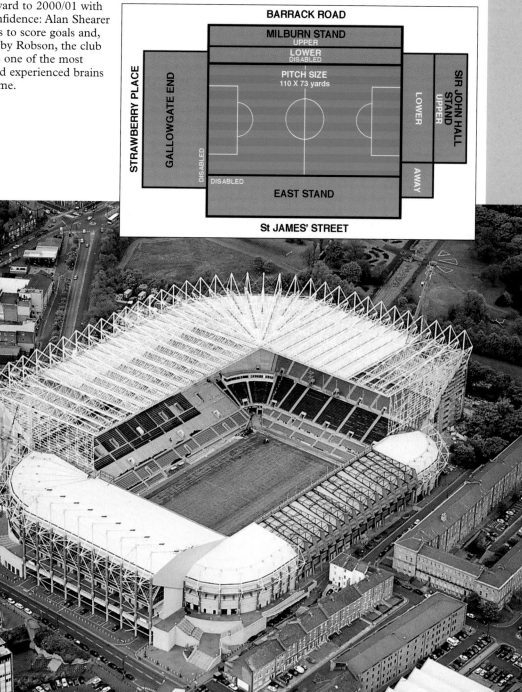

BARRACK ROAD

MILBURN STAND
UPPER
LOWER
DISABLED

STRAWBERRY PLACE

GALLOWGATE END

PITCH SIZE
110 X 73 yards

DISABLED

DISABLED

SIR JOHN HALL STAND

LOWER

UPPER

AWAY

EAST STAND

St JAMES' STREET

NORTHAMPTON TOWN

Sixfields Stadium, Northampton, NN5 5QA

Tel No: 01604 757773
Advance Tickets Tel No: 01604 588338
Fax: 01604 751613
Web Site: www.ntfc.co.uk
League: 2nd Division
Brief History: Founded 1897. Former, County, Ground was part of Northamptonshire County Cricket Ground. Moved to Sixfields Stadium during early 1994/95 season. Record attendance 24,523 (at County Ground); 7,557 (at Sixfields)
(Total) Current Capacity: 7,653 (all seated)

Visiting Supporters' Allocation: 1,277 (all seated)
Club Colours: Claret with white sleeved shirts, white shorts
Nearest Railway Station: Northampton Castle
Parking (Car): Adjacent to Ground
Parking (Coach/Bus): Adjacent to Ground
Police Force and Tel No: Northants (01604 33221)
Disabled Visitors' Facilities:
   Wheelchairs: Available on all four sides
   Blind: Available

KEY
- **C** Club Offices
- **S** Club Shop
- **E** Entrance(s) for visiting supporters
- **R** Refreshment bars for visiting supporters
- **T** Toilets for visiting supporters

↑ North direction (approx)

❶ Weedon Road to Town Centre and Northampton Castle BR station (two miles)
❷ Upton Way, to M1 Junction 15A
❸ A45, to M1 Junction 16
❹ Car parks

Relegated at the end of 1998/99, the Cobblers were one of the pre-season favourites to achieve automatic promotion from the Third Division. Under Ian Atkins, who was probably fortunate to retain the managership after the disaster of the previous season, the club ensured Second Division football in 2000/01 by squeezing Darlington out of the frame on the last day of the season. Victory away at Torquay — itself a team harbouring aspirations of the Play-Offs — ensured that Town retained third spot and consigned the Quakers to the Play-Offs. However, recent precedents would indicate that, unless the team is fortunate, the new season's campaign in the Second Division is likely to be difficult with a further relegation being a very real possibility.

NORWICH CITY

Carrow Road, Norwich, NR1 1JE

Tel No: 01603 760760
Advance Tickets Tel No: 01603 761661
Fax: 01603 613886
Web Site: www.canaries.co.uk
E-Mail: ncfc.corporate@netcom.co.uk
League: 1st Division
Brief History: Founded 1902. Former grounds: Newmarket Road and the Nest, Rosary Road; moved to Carrow Road in 1935. Founder-members 3rd Division (1920). Record attendance 43,984
(Total) Current Capacity: 21,414 (seated)
Visiting Supporters' Allocation: 1,741 (South Stand Blocks F, G, H)

Club Colours: Yellow with green side panel shirts, green shorts
Nearest Railway Station: Norwich
Parking (Car): City centre car parks
Parking (Coach/Bus): Lower Clarence Road
Police Force and Tel No: Norfolk (01603 621212)
Disabled Visitors' Facilities:
  Wheelchairs: South Stand (heated)
  Blind: Commentary available
Anticipated Development(s): The next stage in the redevelopment of Carrow Road will involve the reconstruction of the South Stand, but there is as yet no timescale for this work.

KEY

C Club Offices
S Club Shop
E Entrance(s) for visiting supporters

↑ North direction (approx)

❶ Carrow Road
❷ A47 King Street
❸ River Wensum
❹ Riverside
❺ Car Park
❻ Norwich BR Station

Despite being controlled by celebrity cook Delia Smith, whose usual Midas touch can turn the fortunes of most unlikely products, the Canaries refused to fly up the First Division. A position of mid-table mediocrity — some 20 points off even a Play-Off position — meant that manager Bruce Rioch's fate was sealed even before the season's close, being replaced by Bryan Hamilton. With local rivals Ipswich Town making promotion into the Premiership, fans of City must be hoping that the team can raise their expectations and, at the very least, threaten a Play-Off position in 2000/01.

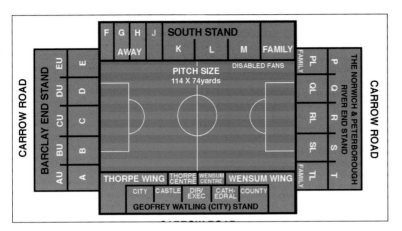

NOTTINGHAM FOREST

City Ground, Nottingham, NG2 5FJ

Tel No: 0115 982 4444
Advance Tickets Tel No: 0115 982 4445
Fax: 0115 982 4455
Web Site: http://www.nottinghamforest.co.uk
E-Mail: info@nottinghamforest.co.uk
League: 1st Division
Brief History: Founded 1865 as Forest Football Club, changed name to Nottingham Forest (c1879). Former Grounds: Forest Recreation Ground, Meadow Cricket Ground, Trent Bridge (Cricket Ground), Parkside, Gregory Ground and Town Ground, moved to City Ground in 1898. Founder-members of Second Division (1892). Record attendance 49,945

(Total) Current Capacity: 30,602 (all seated)
Visiting Supporters' Allocation: Approx 4,750
Club Colours: Red shirts, white shorts
Nearest Railway Station: Nottingham Midland
Parking (Car): East car park and street parking
Parking (Coach/Bus): East car park
Police Force and Tel No: Nottinghamshire (0115 948 1888)
Disabled Visitors' Facilities:
  Wheelchairs: Front of Executive Stand
  Blind: No special facility

KEY

C Club Offices
S Club Shop
E Entrance(s) for visiting supporters

⬆ North direction (approx)

❶ Radcliffe Road
❷ Lady Bay Bridge Road
❸ Trent Bridge
❹ Trent Bridge Cricket Ground
❺ Notts County F.C.
❻ River Trent
❼ Nottingham Midland BR Station (½ mile)

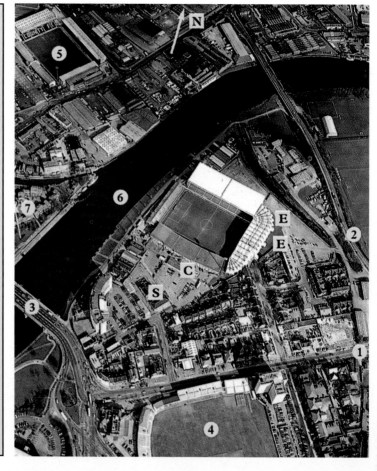

Following the trauma of relegation from the Premier League, Forest entered the First Division under the management of David Platt, whose only managerial experience had been a somewhat disastrous spell at Sampdoria. If that bode ill for the future, the club could at least look at the success of Sunderland in making a storming return to the Premier League as an inspiration. In the event, it was Platt at Sampdoria rather than Reid at Sunderland that marked Forest's First Division career and, instead of fulfilling pre-season expectations of an immediate return to the Premier League, the club was caught in the battle to avoid the drop to the Second Division. With the Premier League 'umbrella' ending at the end of 2000/01, the team has another season to engineer promotion. In a First Division that is likely to be as competitive as ever — with Wednesday, Wimbledon and Watford providing stiff competition to the also-rans of 1999/2000 — Forest will have to achieve a dramatic improvement if the First Division isn't to be the club's fate for 2001/02.

RIVER TRENT

TRENT END STAND
UPPER
LOWER

P

UPPER
EXECUTIVE STAND
LOWER

PITCH SIZE
112 X 78 yards

DISABLED FANS

LOWER
AWAY
UPPER
BRIDGFORD STAND

COLWICK ROAD

MAIN STAND

NOTTS COUNTY

Meadow Lane, Nottingham, NG2 3HJ

Tel No: 0115 952 9000
Advance Tickets Tel No: 0115 955 7210
Fax: 0115 955 3994
Web Site: www.nottscountyfc.co.uk
E-Mail: info@nottscountyfc.co.uk
League: 2nd Division
Brief History: Founded 1862 (oldest club in Football League) as Nottingham, changed to Notts County in c1882. Former Grounds: Notts Cricket Ground (Beeston), Castle Cricket Ground, Trent Bridge Cricket Ground, moved to Meadow Lane in 1910. Founder-members Football League (1888). Record attendance 47,310

(Total) Current Capacity: 20,300 (seated)
Visiting Supporters' Allocation: 5,438 (seated)
Club Colours: Black and white striped shirts, black shorts
Nearest Railway Station: Nottingham Midland
Parking (Car): Mainly street parking
Parking (Coach/Bus): Cattle market
Police Force and Tel No: Nottingham (0115 948 1888)
Disabled Visitors' Facilities:
 Wheelchairs: Meadow Lane/Jimmy Sirrel/Derek Pavis Stands
 Blind: No special facility

KEY

C Club Offices
S Club Shop
E Entrance(s) for visiting supporters
R Refreshment bars for visiting supporters
T Toilets for visiting supporters

↑ North direction (approx)

❶ A6011 Meadow Lane
❷ County Road
❸ A60 London Road
❹ River Trent
❺ Nottingham Midland BR Station (½ mile)

In a Second Division dominated by seven teams, County finished top of the rest in eighth place — 15 points adrift of the unfortunate Bristol Rovers in seventh. Such was the gap between the teams chasing promotion and Play-Off spots and the rest. One factor in the team's failure to mount a sustained challenge for promotion was the departure of manager Sam Allardyce, who left during the course of the season to take over at Bolton Wanderers. His replacement, Jocky Scott, will face a considerable struggle to lift the team into serious promotion candidates, although the relative weakness of the three relegated teams means that there should not be the same disparity in quality between the top half-dozen and the rest of the division in 2000/01.

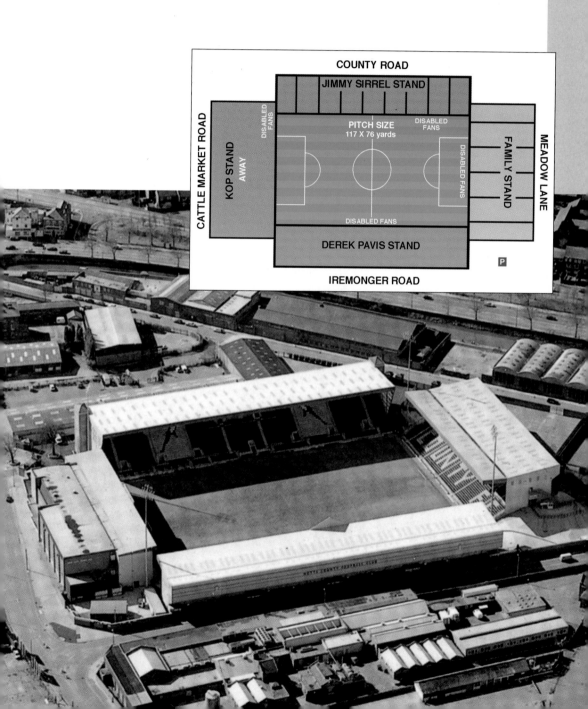

OLDHAM ATHLETIC

Boundary Park, Oldham, OL1 2PA

Tel No: 0161 624 4972
Advance Tickets Tel No: 0161 624 4972
Fax: 0161 627 5915
Web Site: www.oldhamathletic.co.uk
League: 2nd Division
Brief History: Founded 1897 as Pine Villa, changed name to Oldham Athletic in 1899. Former Grounds: Berry's Field, Pine Mill, Athletic Ground (later named Boundary Park), Hudson Fold, moved to Boundary Park in 1906. Record attendance 47,671
(Total) Current Capacity: 13,559 (all seated)
Visiting Supporters' Allocation: 1,800 minimum, 4,600 maximum
Club Colours: Blue shirts, blue shorts
Nearest Railway Station: Oldham Werneth
Parking (Car): Lookers Stand car park

Parking (Coach/Bus): At Ground
Police Force and Tel No: Greater Manchester (0161 624 0444)
Disabled Visitors' Facilities:
  Wheelchairs: Rochdale Road and Seton Stands
  Blind: No special facility
Anticipated Development(s): The plans for the construction of a new 15,000-seat ground at Clayton Playing Fields in conjunction with the local RLFC club have been abandoned. As a result, Athletic will now seek to redevelop Boundary Park further, with the first phase being the construction of a new two-tier stand, costing £15 million, to replace the Lookers Stand. There is, however, no confirmed timetable for this work at the current time.

KEY

C Club Offices

E Entrance(s) for visiting supporters

↑ North direction (approx)

❶ A663 Broadway
❷ Furtherwood Road
❸ Chadderton Way
❹ To A627(M) and M62
❺ To Oldham Werneth BR Station (1½ miles)
❻ Car Park

Above: 685004; *Right:* 685008

Following the escape from relegation at the end of the 1998/99 season, anything higher than 20th position in the Second Division would be progress for Andy Ritchie's team given that many pundits were forecasting relegation. Although the team struggled on occasions, a final position of 14th was better than many expected and offers the potential for further advancement in 2000/01. It seems strange that a club that recently belonged to the top flight and were unfortunate to lose to Manchester United in an FA Cup semi-final could struggle at such a level, but perhaps the success of fellow Lancashire teams Preston North End and Burnley can inspire the Latics to promotion in the new season.

OXFORD UNITED

Manor Ground, London Road, Headington, Oxford, OX3 7RS

Tel No: 01865 761503
Advance Tickets Tel No: 01865 761503
(Ext 207)
Fax: 01865 741820
E-mail: oxford-united@community.co.uk
Website: www.oufc.co.uk
League : 2nd Division
Brief History: Founded 1893 as Headington (later Headington United), changed name to Oxford United in 1960. Former Grounds: Britannia Inn Field, Headington Quarry, Wooten's Field, Manor Ground and The Paddocks. The club moved back to the Manor Ground in 1925. Record attendance 22,730. Proposed move to a new ground currently under construction has stalled
(Total) Current Capacity: 9,650 (6,769 seated)
Visiting Supporters' Allocation: 2,649
Club Colours: Yellow with navy blue trim shirts and navy with yellow trim shorts

Nearest Railway Station: Oxford (three miles)
Parking (Car): Street Parking
Parking (Coach/Bus): Headley Way
Police Force and Tel No: Thames Valley (01865 777501)
Disabled Visitors' Facilities:
  Wheelchairs: Main Stand
  Blind: No special facility
Anticipated Development(s): As is evident with the recent photograph shown here, there has been little progress on the Minchery Farm ground. It was reported after the end of the 1999/2000 season that a meeting, due to be held in mid-July 2000, where the idea of incorporating a multi-screen cinema on the site, would determine further progress. It is unlikely that the team will move before mid-2001 at the earliest, even if construction does restart.

KEY

C Club Offices
E Entrance(s) for visiting supporters
R Refreshment bars for visiting supporters

↑ North direction (approx)

❶ A420 London Road
❷ Oster Road
❸ To City Centre and Oxford BR Station (3 miles)
❹ To A40 and Ring Road (¾ mile)
❺ Cuckoo Lane

Right: 685015

Following relegation at the end of 1998/99 to the Second Division, it seemed as though United was in free fall for most of the 1999/2000 season with relegation to the Third appearing a real possibility. During the course of a disappointing season, Malcolm Shotton, who had done much to try and keep the team spirit afloat during the ongoing financial struggle, was dismissed. In the event, results towards the end of the season saw United beat the drop by a single point, with Cardiff City taking the fourth relegation spot. As can be seen, progress on the new ground is non-existent and it is difficult to see 2000/01 being anything other another season of struggle for the team.

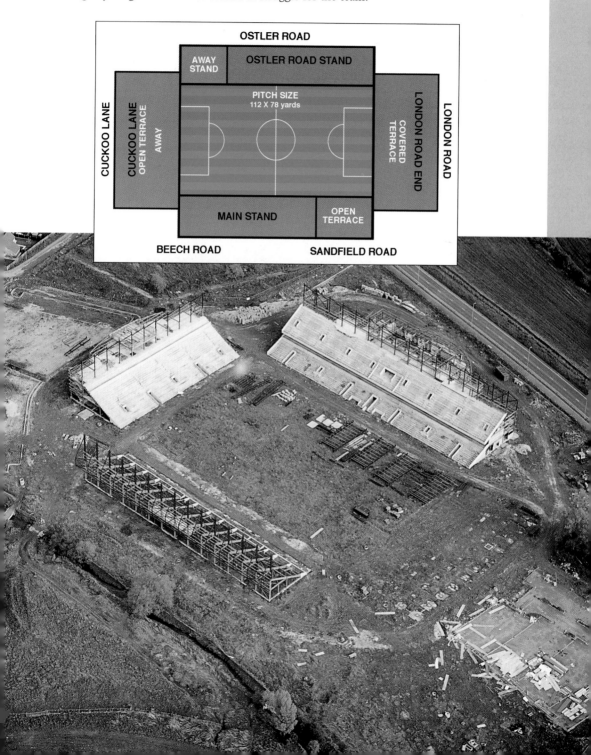

PETERBOROUGH UNITED

London Road, Peterborough, Cambs, PE2 8AL

Tel No: 01733 563947
Advance Tickets Tel No: 01733 563947
Fax: 01733 344140
Web Site: www.theposh.com
E-Mail: football@theposh.com
League: 2nd Division
Brief History: Founded in 1934 (no connection with former 'Peterborough and Fletton United' FC). Elected to Football League in 1960. Record attendance 30,096
(Total) Current Capacity: 13,870 (8,048 seated)
Visiting Supporters' Allocation: 3,758 (756 seated)
Club Colours: Blue shirts, white shorts

Nearest Railway Station: Peterborough
Parking (Car): Peterborough
Parking (Coach/Bus): At ground
Police Force and Tel No: Cambridgeshire (01733 563232
Disabled Visitors' Facilities:
  Wheelchairs: South Stand
  Blind: No special facility
Future Development(s): Following the reroofing of the Moys and London Road ends, long term plans exist for the construction of a new Main Stand — for which plans have been prepared — and other work. However, there is no confirmed timetable for this at present.

KEY

C Club Offices
S Club Shop
E Entrance(s) for visiting supporters
R Refreshment bars for visiting supporters
T Toilets for visiting supporters

↑ North direction (approx)

❶ A15 London Road
❷ Car Parks
❸ Peterborough BR Station (1 mile)
❹ Glebe Road
❺ A605
❻ To A1 (north) (5 miles)
❼ River Nene
❽ To Whittlesey
❾ To A1 (south) (5 miles)

Above: 685033; Right: 685030

One of the pre-season favourites for promotion or the Play-Offs, Barry Fry's Posh fulfilled these expectations by finishing 5th and thus earning a Play-Off semi-final against Fry's erstwhile charges, Barnet. Although the Bees had been soundly beaten 9-1 in one league game in 1998/99, the Play-Offs were always going to be a tighter affair this year, although Posh did eventually battle through to take on Darlington at Wembley in the final. Although facing a Darlington team that dominated the game for long periods, Posh emerged as 1-0 victors, thus bringing back Second Division football to London Road. As with other promoted teams, the euphoria will soon be replaced by the hard reality of trying to maintain this new status in 2000/01.

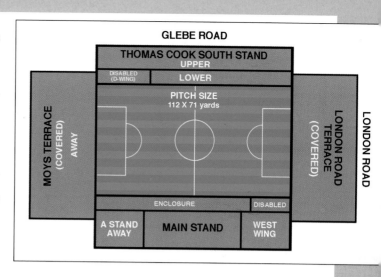

PLYMOUTH ARGYLE

Home Park, Plymouth, PL3 3DQ

Tel No: 01752 562561
Advance Tickets Tel No: 01752 562561
Fax: 01752 606167
Web-site: www.pafc.co.uk
League: 3rd Division
Brief History: Founded 1886 as Argyle Athletic Club, changed name to Plymouth Argyle in 1903. Founder-members Third Division (1920). Record attendance 43,596
(Total) Current Capacity: 19,589 (7,000 seated)
Visiting Supporters' Allocation: 1,990 (120 seated) in Barn Park End and Grandstand (Barn Park Wing)
Club Colours: Green shirts, green shorts

Nearest Railway Station: Plymouth
Parking (Car): Car park adjacent
Parking (Coach/Bus): Central car park
Police Force and Tel No: Devon & Cornwall (01752 701188)
Disabled Visitors' Facilities:
  Wheelchairs: Devonport End
  Blind: Commentary available
Anticipated Development(s): There remain plans for the possible construction of a new 25,000-seat ground closer to the town centre. However, there is nothing definite at this stage and the likelihood is that Argyle will remain at Home Park for the foreseeable future.

KEY

C Club Offices
S Club Shop
E Entrance(s) for visiting supporters
R Refreshment bars for visiting supporters
T Toilets for visiting supporters

↑ North direction (approx)

❶ Outland Road
❷ Car Park
❸ Devonport Road
❹ Central Park
❺ Town Centre & Plymouth BR Station (1/2 mile)

TAVISTOCK ROAD

LYNDHURST STAND

LYNDHURST ROAD

P

DEVONPORT END COVERED

OPEN TERRACE

DISABLED FANS

PITCH SIZE
112 X 72 yards

OPEN PADDOCK

GRANDSTAND

BARN PARK END UNCOVERED TERRACE

AWAY

The Pilgrims' second season back in the Third Division proved to be as difficult for the team as the first, as Kevin Hodges' team finished a disappointing 12th. At least that was a one place improvement on 1998/99 and, at the current rate of progress, fans can be looking to a return to the Second Division by the end of the decade.

PORTSMOUTH

Fratton Park, 57 Frogmore Road, Portsmouth, Hants, PO4 8RA

Tel No: 02392 731204
Advance Tickets Tel No: 02392 861963
Fax: 02392 734129
Web Site: www.pompeyfc.co.uk
E-Mail: pfc@pompey.co.uk
League: 1st Division
Brief History: Founded 1898. Founder-members Third Division (1920). Record attendance 51,385
(Total) Current Capacity: 19,214 (all seated)
  Visiting Supporters' Allocation: 3,121 (max) in Milton Stand
Club Colours: Blue shirts, white shorts
Nearest Railway Station: Fratton

Parking (Car): Street parking
Parking (Coach/Bus): As directed by Police
Police Force and Tel No: Hampshire (02392 321111)
Disabled Visitors' Facilities:
  Wheelchairs: KJC Stand
  Blind: No special facility
Anticipated Development(s): The club has plans for a new 35,000 all-seater stadium to be called the Pompey Centre and this has received local authority approval, although there is not yet a confirmed schedule for if and when this work will be undertaken.

KEY

C Club Offices
S Club Shop
E Entrance(s) for visiting supporters
R Refreshment bars for visiting supporters
T Toilets for visiting supporters

⬆ North direction (approx)

❶ Alverstone Road
❷ Carisbrook Road
❸ A288 Milton Road
❹ A2030 Velder Avenue A27
❺ A2030 Goldsmith Avenue
❻ Fratton BR station (½ mile)
❼ KJC Stand

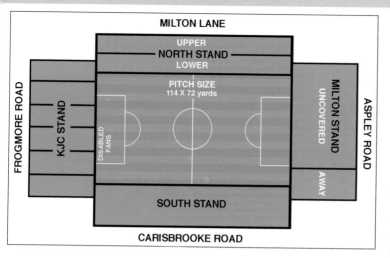

MILTON LANE

UPPER
NORTH STAND
LOWER

PITCH SIZE
114 X 72 yards

FROGMORE ROAD

KJC STAND

DISABLED FANS

MILTON STAND
UNCOVERED

AWAY

ASPLEY ROAD

SOUTH STAND

CARISBROOKE ROAD

Now controlled by the Serbian multi-millionaire Milan Mandaric after a period of financial crisis, Pompey struggled through much of the First Division campaign and were on the fringes of the relegation battle throughout. During the course of the season Alan Ball was replaced by Tony Pulis, who came to the club from Gillingham via a brief stay at Bristol City. Pulis had almost taken the Gills to promotion at the end of 1998/99 but had paid the price for failure in the Play-Off final. His arrival and the promise of significant funds for squad strengthening mean that Pompey fans will be expecting greater rewards than in recent years.

PORT VALE

Vale Park, Burslem, Stoke-on-Trent, ST6 1AW

Tel No: 01782 814134
Advance Tickets Tel No: 01782 811707
Fax: 01782 836875
Web Site: http://port-vale.co.uk
E-Mail: pvfc@port-vale.co.uk
League: 2nd Division
Brief History: Founded 1876 as Burslem Port
Vale, changed name to 'Port Vale' in 1907
(reformed club). Former Grounds: The
Meadows Longport, Moorland Road Athletic
Ground, Cobridge Athletic Grounds,
Recreation Ground Hanley, moved to Vale
Park in 1950. Founder-members Second
Division (1892). Record attendance 48,749
(Total) Current Capacity: 23,500 (all seated)
Visiting Supporters' Allocation: 4,550 (in
Hamil Road Stand)

Club Colours: White shirts, white shorts
Nearest Railway Station: Longport (two miles)
Parking (Car): Car park at Ground
Parking (Coach/Bus): Hamil Road car park
Police Force and Tel No: Staffordshire (01782
577114)
Disabled Visitors' Facilities:
  Wheelchairs: 200 spaces in new Britannic
  Disabled Stand
  Blind: Commentary available
Anticipated Development(s): As can be seen
in the accompanying photographs, work is in
hand for the completion of the new 5,000-seat
capacity Lorne Street Stand. This will
complete work in upgrading Vale Park.

KEY
C Club Offices
S Club Shop
E Entrance(s) for visiting
   supporters

⬆ North direction (approx)

❶ Car Parks
❷ Hamil Road
❸ Lorne Street
❹ To B5051 Moorland Road
❺ To Burslem Town Centre
❻ Railway Stand
❼ Sentinel Stand
❽ Hamil Road Stand
❾ Lorne Street Stand (under
   construction)
❿ Family Section

Above: 685045; Right: 685040

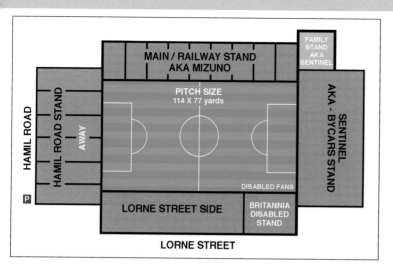

Following their flirtation with relegation in 1998/99, a season during which long-serving (and popular) manager John Rudge was sacked and replaced with Brian Horton, Port Vale went one better and ensured that there will again be local derbies with Stoke City, albeit in the Second Division. Recent years have witnessed considerable expenditure on improving the facilities at Vale Park; no doubt Vale fans would have preferred to see some of that money spent on strengthening the squad in the hope of preserving the club's First Division status.

In the diagram:

HAMIL ROAD

HAMIL ROAD STAND

AWAY

P

MAIN / RAILWAY STAND AKA MIZUNO

PITCH SIZE
114 X 77 yards

FAMILY STAND AKA SENTINEL

SENTINEL AKA - BYCARS STAND

DISABLED FANS

LORNE STREET SIDE

BRITANNIA DISABLED STAND

LORNE STREET

PRESTON NORTH END

Deepdale, Sir Tom Finney Way, Preston, PR1 6RU

Tel No: 01772 902020
Advance Tickets Tel No: 01772 902222
Fax: 01772 653266
Web Site: http://prestonnorthend.co.uk
E-Mail: enquiries@prestonnorthend.co.uk
League: 1st Division
Brief History: Founded 1867 as a Rugby Club, changed to soccer in 1881. Former ground: Moor Park, moved to (later named) Deepdale in 1875. Founder-members Football League (1888). Record attendance 42,684
(Total) Current Capacity: 21,363 (14,730 seated)
Visiting Supporters' Allocation: 5,942 maximum
Club Colours: White shirts, blue shorts
Nearest Railway Station: Preston (2 miles)
Parking (Car): West Stand car park
Parking (Coach/Bus): West Stand car park

Police Force and Tel No: Lancashire (01772 203203)
Disabled Visitors' Facilities:
  Wheelchairs: Tom Finney Stand and Bill Shankly Stand
  Blind: Earphones Commentary
Anticipated Development(s): Following completion of the new Bill Shankly Stand (named after the former Preston player and Liverpool Manager), which replaced the old Kop Stand (Fulwood End), work will next commence on replacing the Pavilion Stand. Shortly after achieving the Second Division title, PNE announced that the club would be seeking to raise £7.5 million to fund the completion of work on Deepdale and to strengthen the squad for First Division football. There is, as yet, no confirmed timetable for the work required on the ground.

KEY

C Club Offices

↑ North direction (approx)

❶ A6033 Deepdale Road
❷ Lawthorpe Road
❸ Car Park
❹ A5085 Blackpool Road
❺ Preston BR Station (2 miles)
❻ Bill Shankly Stand
❼ Tom Finney Stand

A triumphant season for one of the traditional great names of English football saw Preston North End under the astute management of David Moyes achieve the Second Division championship and thus promotion to the First Division, reaching this level for the first time in almost two decades. In the 19 years since First (old Second) Division football was last played at Deepdale the ground has been radically altered with both the Tom Finney and Bill Shankly stands. With the faces of these two great figures from the team's past staring down from the eponymous stands, fans will be hoping that some of their magic will rub off on the team as it faces the difficult task of cementing its First Division status.

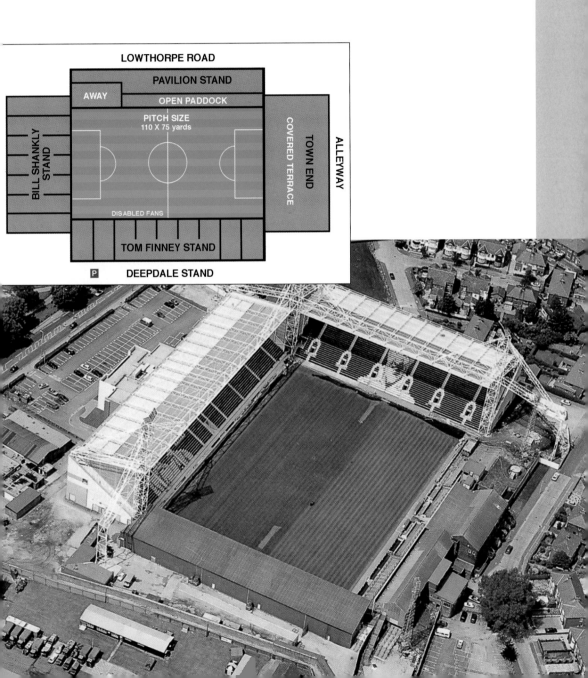

LOWTHORPE ROAD

PAVILION STAND

AWAY

OPEN PADDOCK

PITCH SIZE
110 X 75 yards

BILL SHANKLY STAND

COVERED TERRACE

TOWN END

ALLEYWAY

DISABLED FANS

TOM FINNEY STAND

P   DEEPDALE STAND

QUEENS PARK RANGERS

Loftus Road Stadium, South Africa Road, London, W12 7PA

Tel No: 020 8743 0262
Advance Tickets Tel No: 020 8740 2575
Fax: 020 8749 0994
Web Site: www.qpr.co.uk
League: 1st Division
Brief History: Founded 1885 as 'St. Jude's Institute', amalgamated with Christchurch Rangers to become Queens Park Rangers in 1886. Football League record number of former Grounds and Ground moves (13 different venues, 17 changes), including White City Stadium (twice) final move to Loftus Road in 1963. Founder-members Third Division (1920). Record attendance (at Loftus Road) 35,353
(Total) Current Capacity: 19,148 (all seated)
Visiting Supporters' Allocation: 3,100

Club Colours: Blue and white hooped shirts, white shorts
Nearest Railway Station: Shepherds Bush and White City (both tube)
Parking (Car): White City NCP and street parking
Parking (Coach/Bus): White City NCP
Police Force and Tel No: Metropolitan (020 8246 7255)
Disabled Visitors' Facilities:
  Wheelchairs: Ellerslie Road Stand and West Paddock
  Blind: Ellerslie Road Stand
Anticipated Development(s): There is vague talk of possible relocation, but nothing has been confirmed. Given the constrained site occupied by Loftus Road, it will be difficult to increase the existing ground's capacity.

KEY
C Club Offices
S Club Shop
E Entrance(s) for visiting supporters

↑ North direction (approx)

❶ South Africa Road
❷ To White City Tube Station, A219 Wood Lane and A40 Western Avenue
❸ A420 Uxbridge Road
❹ To Shepherds Bush Tube Station
❺ Ellerslie Road
❻ BBC Television Centre
❼ Loftus Road
❽ Bloemfontein Road

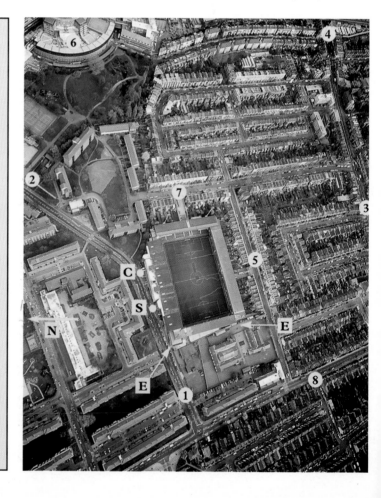

With the Premier League's financial 'umbrella' now long departed and financial difficulties preventing a massive strengthening of the squad, 1999/2000 was always going to be a season of consolidation for Rangers, particularly after two seasons where relegation to the Second Division rather than promotion to the Premier League was more likely. In the event, Rangers had, by recent form, a good season, finishing 10th in the First Division. Whilst never threatening a Play-Off place seriously, there are serious grounds for optimism at Loftus Road if manager Gerry Francis can continue to work successfully with his squad.

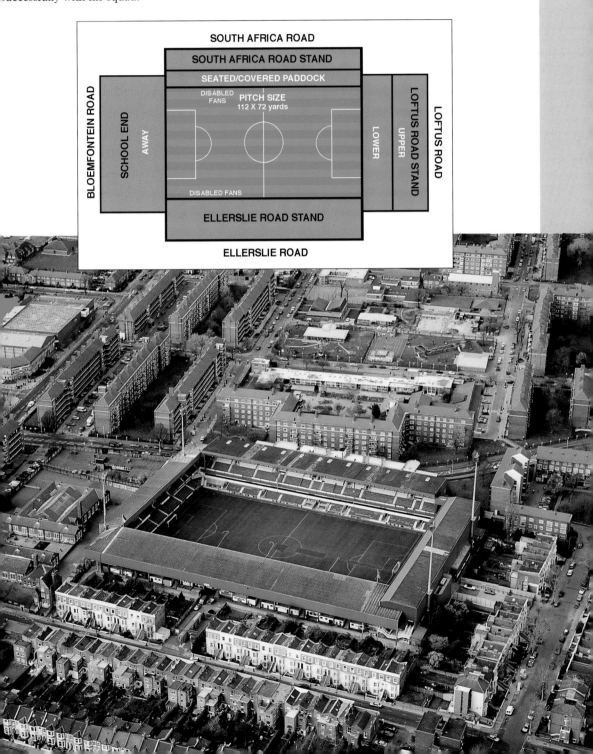

READING

Madejski Stadium, Bennet Road, Reading, RG2 0FL

Tel No: 0118 968 1100
Advance Tickets Tel No: 0118 968 1000
Fax: 0118 968 1101
Web Site: www.readingfc.co.uk
E-Mail: comments@readingfc.co.uk
League: 2nd Division
Brief History: Founded 1871. Amalgamated with Reading Hornets in 1877 and with Earley in 1889. Former Grounds: Reading Recreation Ground, Reading Cricket Ground, Coley Park, Caversham Cricket Cround and Elm Park (1895-1998); moved to the Madejski Stadium at the start of the 1998/99 season. Founder-members of the Third Division in 1920. Record attendance (at Elm Park) 33,042; (at Madejski Stadium) 20,055
(Total) Current Capacity: 24,200 (all seated)
Visiting Supporters' Allocation: 4,300

(maximum in the South Stand)
Club Colours: White with blue hoops shirts, white shorts
Nearest Railway Station: Reading (2.5 miles)
Parking (Car): 1,800-space car park at the ground, 700 of these spaces are reserved
Parking (Coach/Bus): As directed
Police Force and Tel No: Thames Valley (0118 953 6000)
Disabled Visitors' Facilities:
　Wheelchairs: 128 designated spaces on all four sides of the ground
　Blind: 12 places for match day commentaries
Anticipated Development(s): The club has plans, if the need arises, to add an addition 5,000-seat section to the East Stand.

KEY

C Club Offices
S Club Shop

↑ North direction (approx)

❶ North Stand
❷ East Stand
❸ South Stand (away)
❹ West Stand
❺ Reading Stadium
❻ A33 Basingstoke Road
❼ To Reading town centre and station (two miles)
❽ M4 Junction (J11)
❾ Link Road to A33
❿ A33 southbound
⓫ M4 westbound (towards Swindon)
⓬ M4 eastbound (towards London)

138　　*Above: 679494; Right: 679490*

WEST STAND
UPPER
LOWER
PITCH SIZE
102 X 70 metres

SOUTH STAND
AWAY

NORTH STAND

EAST STAND

ACRE ROAD

With a state-of-the-art stadium and a team not quite of the same standard, Reading faced another season of Second Division football. Widely tipped to make the Play-Offs, Tommy Burns's team failed to fire on most (any?) cylinders during the course of 1999/2000 and finishing tenth — some 20 points off Stoke City in sixth place and an advance of only one place on the disastrous 1998/99 result — was a major disappointment. With a capacity of more than 24,000 the Madejski Stadium ought to be playing host to First Division football; unfortunately, unless the team's fortunes change dramatically — which seems unlikely (but you never know) — another season of mid-table mediocrity in the Second Division seems an odds on certainty.

ROCHDALE

Willbutts Lane, Spotland, Rochdale, OL11 5DS

Tel No: 01706 644648
Advance Tickets Tel No: 01706 644648
Fax: 01706 648466
Web-site: www.rochdaleafc.co.uk
E-Mail: club@rochdale-football-club.co.uk
League: 3rd Division
Brief History: Founded 1907 from former Rochadale Town F.C. (founded 1900). Founder-members Third Division North (1921). Record attendance 24,231
(Total) Current Capacity: 10,262 (8,342 seated) following completion of Pearl Street Stand
Visiting Supporters' Allocation: 3,650 (seated) in Willbutts Lane Stand
Club Colours: Blue shirts, blue shorts

Nearest Railway Station: Rochdale
Parking (Car): Rear of ground
Parking (Coach/Bus): Rear of ground
Police Force and Tel No: Greater Manchester (01706 647401)
Disabled Visitors' Facilities:
  Wheelchairs: Main stand – disabled area
  Blind: Commentary available
Anticipated Development(s): Work is progressing on the construction of a new 3,650-seat stand to replace the Willbutts Lane Terrace. Whilst work is in progress, away fans will be allocated 650 seats in the Main Stand. It is hoped that the new facility will be open on 15 September 2000, when the away capacity at Spotland will be increased to 3,650.

KEY

C Club Offices
S Club Shop
E Entrance(s) for visiting supporters

⬆ North direction (approx)

❶ Willbutts Lane
❷ A627 Edenfield Road
❸ Rochdale BR Station (½ mile)
❹ Sandy Lane
❺ To M62
❻ To M65 and North
❼ Pearl Street Stand

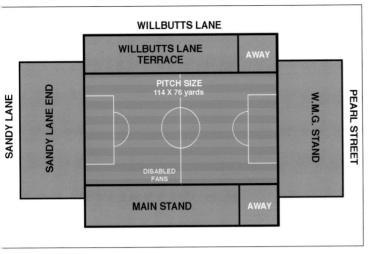

WILLBUTTS LANE

| SANDY LANE | SANDY LANE END | WILLBUTTS LANE TERRACE | AWAY | W.M.G. STAND | PEARL STREET |

PITCH SIZE
114 X 76 yards

DISABLED FANS

MAIN STAND | AWAY

Following his resignation as manager of Mansfield at the end of the 1998/99 season, Steve Parkin moved to Spotland and had the satisfaction of seeing his new charges progress well in the Third Division and finish higher than the Stags. Finishing in 10th place was an achievement and, if the team continues to make similar progress, fans can look forward to a season of some promise. Automatic promotion may well be beyond the team, but a challenge for the Play-Offs should be within range.

ROTHERHAM UNITED

Millmoor Ground, Rotherham, S60 1HR

Tel No: 01709 512434
Advance Tickets Tel No: 01709 512434
Fax: 01709 512762
Web Site: www.themillers.co.uk
League: 2nd Division
Brief History: Founded 1877 (as Thornhill later Thornhill United), changed name to Rotherham County in 1905 and to Rotherham United in 1925 (amalgamated with Rotherham Town – Football League members 1893-97 – in 1925). Former Grounds include: Red House Ground and Clifton Lane Cricket Ground, moved to Millmoor in 1907. Record attendance 25,000
(Total) Current Capacity: 11,533 (4,486 seated)
Visiting Supporters' Allocation: 2,155 (all seated) in Railway End

Club Colours: Red shirts, white shorts
Nearest Railway Station: Rotherham Central
Parking (Car): Kimberworth and Main Street car parks, plus large car park adjacent to ground
Parking (Coach/Bus): As directed by Police
Police Force and Tel No: South Yorkshire (01709 371121)
Disabled Visitors' Facilities:
  Wheelchairs: Millmoor Lane
  Blind: Commentary available
Anticipated Developments(s): The club has plans for the redevelopment of Millmoor, starting with the construction of a new Millmoor Lane Stand to be followed by a new Main Stand. There is, however, no confirmed schedule for this work.

KEY

C Club Offices
S Club Shop
E Entrance(s) for visiting supporters
R Refreshment bars for visiting supporters
T Toilets for visiting supporters

↑ North direction (approx)

❶ Car Park
❷ Rotherham Central BR Station
❸ A6109 Masborough Road
❹ Millmoor Lane
❺ To A6178 and M1 Junction 34

After the disappointment of failure in the Play-Offs at the end of the 1998/99 season, the Millers decided to improve matters and not leave things to chance, by taking the second automatic promotion spot from the Third Division. Failure to defeat Swansea City at home in the final game of the season meant that the championship went to South Wales; however, the day's events were marred by the death of a fan, who was fatally injured by a police horse. Thus, after a gap of a couple of years, Second Division football will return to Millmoor. Ronnie Moore and his team will, however, have seen that two of the teams promoted at the end of 1998/99 — Cardiff City and Scunthorpe United — were immediately relegated back to the Third Division and Cambridge United looked a certainty to join them for much of the year. Fans of the Millers can expect a season where their hopes must be that there at least four worse teams in the division.

SCUNTHORPE UNITED

Glanford Park, Doncaster Road, Scunthorpe DN15 8TD

Tel No: 01724 848077
Advance Tickets Tel No: 01724 848077
Fax: 01724 857986
Web Site: www.scunthorpe-united.co.uk
League: 3rd Division
Brief History: Founded 1899 as Scunthorpe United, amalgamated with North Lindsey to become 'Scunthorpe & Lindsey United' in 1912. Changed name to Scunthorpe United in 1956. Former Grounds: Crosby (Lindsey United) and Old Showground, moved to Glanford Park in 1988. Elected to Football League in 1950. Record attendance 8,775 (23,935 at Old Showground)
(Total) Current Capacity: 9,200 (6,400 seated)
Visiting Supporters' Allocation: 1,678

Club Colours: White shirts with claret and blue trim, white shorts
Nearest Railway Station: Scunthorpe
Parking (Car): At ground
Parking (Coach/Bus): At ground
Police Force and Tel No: Humberside (01724 282888)
Disabled Visitors' Facilities:
 Wheelchairs: GMB Stand
 Blind: Commentary available
Anticipated Development(s): Although a new stadium – Glanford Park opened in 1988 – there is a possibility that, in the future, the existing Evening Telegraph Stand will be demolished and replaced by a two-tier structure.

KEY

C Club Offices
S Club Shop
E Entrance(s) for visiting supporters
R Refreshment bars for visiting supporters
T Toilets for visiting supporters

↑ North direction (approx)

❶ Car Park
❷ Glanford Stand
❸ A18 Scunthorpe BR Station and Town Centre (1½ miles)
❹ M181 and M180 Junction 3

Above: 612994; Right: 612992

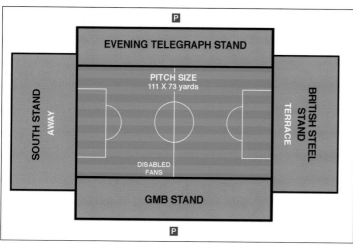

P

EVENING TELEGRAPH STAND

PITCH SIZE
111 X 73 yards

SOUTH STAND
AWAY

BRITISH STEEL
STAND
TERRACE

DISABLED
FANS

GMB STAND

P

Promoted through the Play-Offs at the end of 1998/99, United were widely recognised as being amongst the potential strugglers in the Second Division in 1999/2000. In this, fans were not to be disappointed, although the fact that the team failed to survive will be seen as a disaster. With manager Brian Laws still in place fans will be expecting the team to make the Play-Offs at worst.

SHEFFIELD UNITED

Bramall Lane, Sheffield, S2 4SU

Tel No: 0114 221 5757
Advance Tickets Tel No: 0114 221 1889
Fax: 0114 272 3030
Web Site: http://www.sheffutd.co.uk
E-Mail: info@sufc.co.uk
League: 1st Division
Brief History: Founded 1889. (Sheffield
   Wednesday occasionally used Bramall Lane
   c1880.) Founder-members 2nd Division
   (1892). Record attendance 68,287
(Total) Current Capacity: 30,370 (all seated)
Visiting Supporters' Allocation: 2,063 (seated)
Club Colours: Red and white striped shirts,
   black shorts

Nearest Railway Station: Sheffield Midland
Parking (Car): Street parking
Parking (Coach/Bus): As directed by Police
Police Force and Tel No: South Yorkshire
   (0114 276 8522)
Disabled Visitors' Facilities:
   Wheelchairs: John Street South Stand
   Blind: Commentary available
Anticipated Development(s): None planned
   following the completion of the John Street
   Stand.

KEY
C Club Offices
S Club Shop
E Entrance(s) for visiting
   supporters

↑ North direction (approx)

❶ A621 Bramall Lane
❷ Shoreham Street
❸ Car Park
❹ Sheffield Midland BR
   Station (1/4 mile)
❺ John Street
❻ Spion Kop
❼ John Street Stand

With the departure of Steve Bruce to ambitious Huddersfield Town during the close season, new manager Adrian Heath proved to be short-term incumbent of the Bramall Lane hot seat. Leaving during the course of the season, he was replaced by Neil Warnock. Although he arrived too late to reverse the team's fortunes — and 16th place was a disappointment after the team had been threatening for promotion in previous years — his arrival will give fans increased optimism for the start of the new campaign. Moreover, with Wednesday's relegation, there will be a greater edge to the First Division in 2000/01.

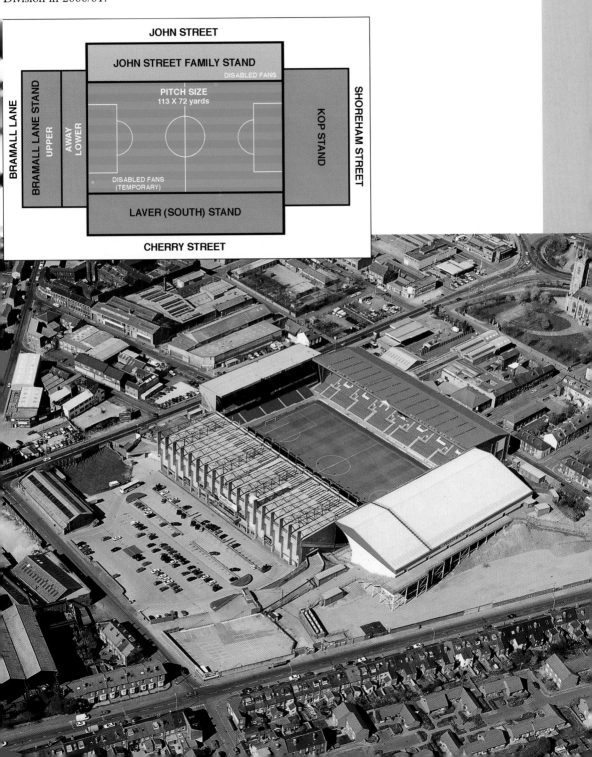

JOHN STREET

JOHN STREET FAMILY STAND

DISABLED FANS

PITCH SIZE
113 X 72 yards

BRAMALL LANE

BRAMALL LANE STAND

UPPER

AWAY
LOWER

DISABLED FANS
(TEMPORARY)

LAVER (SOUTH) STAND

KOP STAND

SHOREHAM STREET

CHERRY STREET

SHEFFIELD WEDNESDAY

Hillsborough, Sheffield, S6 1SW

Tel No: 0114 221 2121
Advance Tickets Tel No: 0114 221 2400
Fax: 0114 221 2122
Web Site: http://swfc.co.uk
E-Mail: enquiries@swfc.co.uk
League: 1st Division
Brief History: Founded 1867 as The
Wednesday F.C. (changed to Sheffield
Wednesday c1930). Former Grounds: London
Road, Wyrtle Road (Heeley), Sheaf House
Ground, Encliffe & Olive Grove (Bramall Lane
also used occasionally), moved to Hillsborough
(then named 'Owlerton' in 1899). Founder-
members Second Division (1892). Record
attendance 72,841

(Total) Current Capacity: 39,184 (all seated)
Visiting Supporters' Allocation: 3,900 (all
seated) in West Stand Upper
Club Colours: Blue and white striped shirts,
blue shorts
Nearest Railway Station: Sheffield (4 miles)
Parking (Car): Street Parking
Parking (Coach/Bus): Owlerton Stadium
Police Force and Tel No: South Yorkshire
(0114 234 3131)
Disabled Visitors' Facilities:
Wheelchairs: North and Lower West Stands
Blind: Commentary available

KEY

C Club Offices
S Club Shop
E Entrance(s) for visiting
supporters

↑ North direction (approx)

❶ Leppings Lane
❷ River Don
❸ A61 Penistone Road North
❹ Sheffield BR Station and
City Centre (4 miles)
❺ Spion Kop
❻ To M1 (North)
❼ To M1 (South)
❽ West Stand

Above: 612713; *Right:* 612718

A highly disappointing season for Wednesday saw the team criticised by local MPs, Danny Wilson depart as manager and ultimately relegation to the First Division after nearly a decade of top flight football. A poor start to the season meant that the team was always chasing safety and, despite odd good results (notably the double over fellow strugglers Wimbledon) which might have lifted a team that did possess some talent, it looked a foregone conclusion that Wednesday would be relegated for much of the season. With relegation, there will, no doubt, be some departures from the squad, but with others, such as the talented Alan Quinn, pledging their future to the Owls, fans will be expecting an immediate return to the Premier League. With Barnsley, Huddersfield and Sheffield United also all in the First Division, there will be no end of local derbies for Wednesday in 2000/01, although most fans would have been happy to have miss these in preference for matches against the Uniteds of Leeds and Manchester under new manager Paul Jewell.

SHREWSBURY TOWN

Gay Meadow, Shrewsbury, SY2 6AB

Tel No: 01743 360111
Advance Tickets Tel No: 01743 360111
Fax: 01743 236384
Web Site: www.shrewsburytown.co.uk
League: 3rd Division
Brief History: Founded 1886. Former Gounds: Monkmoor Racecourse, Ambler's Field & The Barracks Ground (moved to Gay Meadow in 1910). Elected to Football League in 1950. Record attendance 18,917
(Total) Current Capacity: 8,000 (4,000 seated)
Visiting Supporters' Allocation: 2,000 (500 seated)
Club Colours: Blue and amber striped shirts, blue and amber shorts
Nearest Railway Station: Shrewsbury
Parking (Car): Adjacent car park
Parking (Coach/Bus): Gay Meadow

Police Force and Tel No: West Mercia (01743 232888)
Disabled Visitors' Facilities:
  Wheelchairs: Alongside pitch (as directed)
  Blind: No special facility
Anticipated Development(s): The club is still hoping to construct a new stadium. It was hoped that this new stadium, costing some £8.5 million would provide seats for some 10,000, would be completed in time for the start of the 2000/01 season. However, planning consent for the new ground and for any linked redevelopment of the existing Gay Meadow site has yet to be given. Until outstanding issues are resolved it is unlikely that the club will be able to contemplate work on the new stadium and thus the Gay Meadow is likely to be home for the Shrews for at least another season.

KEY

C Club Offices
S Club Shop
E Entrance(s) for visiting supporters
R Refreshment bars for visiting supporters
T Toilets for visiting supporters

↑ North direction (approx)

❶ Entrance road to ground
❷ Abbey Foregate
❸ River Severn
❹ Car Parks
❺ Shrewsbury BR Station (1 mile – shortest route)
❻ Riverside Terrace
❼ English Bridge
❽ Wyle Cop
❾ Station End (away)
❿ Wakeman End
⓫ Wakeman/Centre/Station Stand
⓬ Old Potts Way (all routes via ring road)

Above: 679527; Right: 679522

It was a nerve-wracking season for fans of the Shrews. With manager Jake King replaced by Kevin Ratcliffe, the former Everton and Wales star, during the course of the season, the team was rooted to last spot in the Third Division at the start of the final day and facing the very real prospect of relegation to the Conference. Needing to beat Exeter City at St James' Park and relying on results elsewhere, the Shrews achieved a notable 2-1 win which consigned Chester — ironically Ratcliffe's former club — to relegation. However, unless there is a considerable change in playing fortunes in 2000/01, it is hard to see the new season offering the team anything other than another struggle to beat the drop.

RIVER SEVERN

RIVERSIDE TERRACE
COVERED TERRACE

PITCH SIZE
116 X 75 yards

ABBEY FOREGATE

WAKEMAN END

STATION END
(PART COVERED TERRACE)
AWAY

DISABLED FANS

DISABLED FANS

MAIN STAND

STATION STAND AWAY

P

SOUTHAMPTON

The Dell, Milton Road, Southampton, SO15 2XH

Tel No: 02380 220505
Advance Tickets Tel No: 02380 22857 5
  or 02380 3371717. **Fax:** 02380 330360
Web Site: www.saintsfc.co.uk
E-Mail: sfc@tcp.co.uk
League: F.A. Premier
Brief History: Founded 1885 as 'Southampton
  St. Mary's Young Men's Association' (changed
  name to Southampton in 1897). Former
  Grounds: Northlands Road, Antelope Ground,
  County Ground, moved to The Dell in 1898.
  Founder-members Third Division (1920).
  Record attendance 31,044
(Total) Current Capacity: 15,250 (all seated)
Visiting Supporters' Allocation: 1,500 (all seated)
Club Colours: Red and white shirts, black shorts
Nearest Railway Station: Southampton
Parking (Car): Street parking

Parking (Coach/Bus): As directed by Police
Police Force and Tel No: Hampshire (02380
  581111)
Disabled Visitors' Facilities:
  Wheelchairs: Milton Road (book in advance)
  Blind: Commentary available (book in
  advance)
Anticipated Development(s): The club was
  granted planning permission in early 1999 for
  the construction of a new 32,000-seat ground
  at Britannia Road in St Mary's. It is hoped that
  this ground will be available for the start of the
  2001/02 season and will mean that
  Southampton will no longer possess the
  ground with the smallest capacity in the
  Premiership (assuming, of course, that the
  club's annual battle against relegation is again
  successful).

KEY

C Club Offices
S Club Shop
E Entrance(s) for visiting
  supporters
R Refreshment bars for visiting
  supporters
T Toilets for visiting supporters

⬆ North direction (approx)

❶ Archers Road
❷ Milton Road
❸ Hill Lane
❹ To Southampton BR station
❺ To A33, M3 and the north

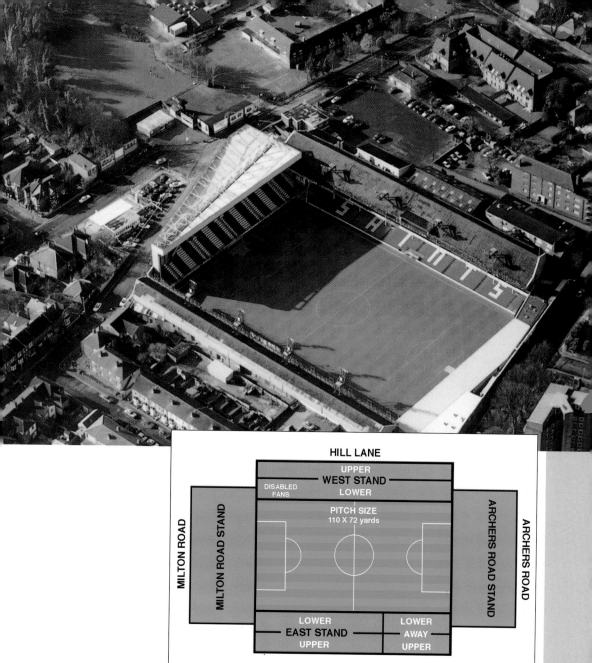

HILL LANE

UPPER
WEST STAND
LOWER

DISABLED FANS

PITCH SIZE
110 X 72 yards

MILTON ROAD

MILTON ROAD STAND

ARCHERS ROAD STAND

ARCHERS ROAD

LOWER
EAST STAND
UPPER

LOWER
AWAY
UPPER

A curious season for Saints' fans saw the team not directly threatened with last-day relegation — although having a direct impact in the relegation places through the defeat of Wimbledon at The Dell on the last Sunday of the season — and a manager sidelined due to a pending court case. Under new (temporary?) manager Glenn Hoddle, the Saints achieved — unusually — Premier League survival a couple of weeks before the season's close and in the diminutive Latvian Marian Pahars had one of the more talented overseas players to emerge in 1999/2000. However, with the Premier League likely to be stronger in 2000/01 than in the last season, most will expect the Saints to be facing another in their regular campaigns to avoid the drop if Premier League football is to be played at the new stadium from August 2001 onwards.

SOUTHEND UNITED

Roots Hall Ground, Victoria Avenue, Southend-on-Sea, SS2 6NQ

Tel No: 01702 304050
Advance Tickets Tel No: 01702 304090
Fax: 01702 330164
League: 3rd Division
Brief History: Founded 1906. Former Grounds: Roots Hall, Kursaal, the Stadium Grainger Road, moved to Roots Hall (new Ground) 1955. Founder-members Third Division (1920). Record attendance 31,033
(Total) Current Capacity: 12,306 (all seated)
Visiting Supporters' Allocation: 3,110 (all seated) in North Stand and North West Enclosure
Club Colours: Blue shirts, blue shorts
Nearest Railway Station: Prittlewell

Parking (Car): Street parking
Parking (Coach/Bus): Car park at Ground
Police Force and Tel No: Essex (01702 431212)
Disabled Visitors' Facilities:
  Wheelchairs: West Stand
  Blind: Commentary available
Anticipated Development(s): It has been reported that Roots Hall has now been sold, although the club has a four-year period of grace before it needs to vacate the site. There are plans for the construction of a new 10,000-seat ground at Eastern Avenue and current plans envisage the club moving to the new ground for the start of the 2002/03 season.

KEY

C Club Offices

E Entrance(s) for visiting supporters

R Refreshment bars for visiting supporters

T Toilets for visiting supporters

↑ North direction (approx)

❶ Director's Car Park
❷ Prittlewell BR Station (1/4 mile)
❸ A127 Victoria Aveneue
❹ Fairfax Drive
❺ Southend centre (1/2 mile)
❻ North Stand

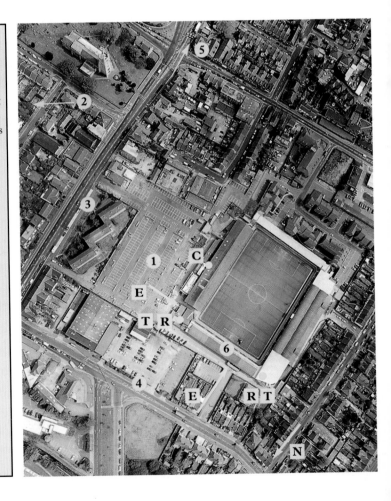

It is surprising how quickly Southend United has fallen from grace. It seems only a couple of years since the team was playing in the First Division and yet, today, the team languishes in the nether regions of the Third Division — finishing 16th in 1999/2000 — and with considerable uncertainty over its future now that the clock is ticking away on its presence at Roots Hall. Now managed by Alan Little, it is difficult to see the team achieve anything more than a position of mid-table mediocrity.

Diagram labels:

SHAKESPEARE DRIVE

WEST STAND

AWAY

ROOTS HALL AVENUE

FRANK WALTON STAND

UPPER TIER

LOWER TIER

DISABLED FANS

PITCH SIZE
110 X 74 yards

NORTH STAND

AWAY

FAIRFAX DRIVE

VISUALLY IMPAIRED

BLACK | GREEN | RED | YELLOW | BLUE

EAST STAND

VICTORIA AVENUE

STOCKPORT COUNTY

Edgeley Park, Hardcastle Road, Edgeley, Stockport, SK3 9DD

Tel No: 0161 286 8888
Advance Tickets Tel No: 0161 286 8888
Fax: 0161 286 8900
Web Site: www.stockportcounty.com
League: 1st Division
Brief History: Founded 1883 as Heaton Norris Rovers, changed name to Stockport County in 1890. Former Grounds: Heaton Norris Recreation Ground, Heaton Norris Wanderers Cricket Ground, Chorlton's Farm, Ash Inn Ground, Wilkes Field (Belmont Street) and Nursery Inn (Green Lane), moved to Edgeley Park in 1902. Record attendance 27,833
(Total) Current Capacity: 11,761 (9,491 seated)
Visiting Supporters' Allocation: 3,615 (964 seated)
Club Colours: Blue with white stripe shirts, blue shorts
Nearest Railway Station: Stockport

Parking (Car): Street Parking
Parking (Coach/Bus): As directed by Police
Police Force and Tel No: Greater Manchester (0161 872 5050)
Disabled Visitors' Facilities:
  Wheelchairs: Main Stand
  Blind: Headsets available
Anticipated Development(s): The club is still planning for the reconstruction of the Railway end, with the intention of construction a new 5,500-seat stand on the site. Although it had been hoped that work would start during the 1999/2000 season this did not occur and an actual time-scale is now not confirmed. After the Railway End is completed, there are tentative plans to upgrade the Vernon BS Stand; this work will ultimately take Edgeley Park to a 20,000 capacity.

KEY

C Club Offices
E Entrance(s) for visiting supporters

↑ North direction (approx)

❶ Mercian Way
❷ Hardcastle Road
❸ Stockport BR station (1/4 mile)
❹ Railway End
❺ Main Stand
❻ Cheadle Stand

156

Despite a prognosis that saw imminent relegation for Andy Kilner's team, the last season started reasonably brightly at Edgeley Park. However, as the season progressed, so an inexorable drift down the First Division table commenced. Ultimately, County finished in 17th spot, well above the drop zone but sufficiently close to it to cause concern for the new season. With ambitious teams like Preston North End and Gillingham coming up — and with some of the weakest teams in the division (most notably Swindon) already relegated — fans of the Hatters would be mad to expect anything other than a battle against relegation in 2000/01.

STOKE CITY

Britannia Stadium, Stanley Matthews Way, Stoke-on-Trent ST4 5EG

Tel No: 01782 592222
Advance Tickets Tel No: 01782 592200
Fax: 01782 592221
League: 2nd Division
Brief History: Founded 1863 as Stoke F.C., amalgamated with Stoke Victoria in 1878, changed to Stoke City in 1925. Former Grounds: Sweetings Field, Victoria Ground (1878-1997), moved to new ground for start of 1997/98 season. Record attendance (at Victoria Ground): 51,380; at Britannia Stadium 26,664
(Total) Current Capacity: 28,353 (all-seater)
Visiting Supporters' Allocation: 5,000 (in the South Stand)
Club Colours: Red and white striped shirts, white shorts

Nearest Railway Station: Stoke-on-Trent
Parking (Car): The 650 parking spaces at the ground are for officials and guests only. The 1,600 spaces in the South car park are pre-booked only, with the majority held by season ticket holders. There is some on-street parking, but with a 10-15min walk.
Parking (Coach/Bus): As directed
Police Force and Tel No: Staffordshire (01782 744644)
Disabled Visitors' Facilities:
  Wheelchairs: 164 places for disabled spectators
  Blind: Commentaries available
Anticipated Development(s): None following the completion of the new ground.

KEY	
↑	North direction (approx)
❶	Victoria Ground (site of)
❷	Stoke BR station
❸	A500 Queensway
❹	North Stand
❺	West Stand
❻	East Stand
❼	South Stand (away)
❽	A50 to Uttoxeter
❾	To M6 northbound
❿	To M6 southbound

As one of the traditional 'big' clubs of the English game, it must cause fans of the Potters considerable distress to see the team's inability to sustain a serious challenge for promotion. It is even more galling in that one of the teams relegated with Stoke at the end of 1997/98 — Manchester City — has now bounced back to promotion to the Premier League. In the season when one of the greatest players from City's past — Sir Stanley Matthews — died, at least the team managed to reach the Play-Offs. Unfortunately, defeat over the two legs by ambitious Gillingham consigned the team to another season of Second Division fare. At least, for the current season, derbies can be resumed with Port Vale. The one bright spot for Potters' fans in 1999/2000 was the relegation of local rivals Port Vale.

SUNDERLAND

Stadium of Light, Sunderland, SR5 1SU

Tel No: 0191 551 5000
Advance Tickets Tel No: 0191 551 5151
Fax: 0191 551 5123
Web Site: www.sunderland-afc.com
League: F.A. Premiership
Brief History: Founded 1879 as 'Sunderland &
District Teachers Association', changed to
'Sunderland Association' in 1880 and shortly
after to 'Sunderland'. Former Grounds: Blue
House Field, Groves Field (Ashbrooke), Horatio
Street, Abbs Field, Newcastle Road and Roker
Park (1898-1997); moved to Stadium of Light for
the start of the 1997/98 season. Record crowd (at
Roker Park): 75,118; at Stadium of Light
(46,346)
(Total) Current Capacity: 47,500 all-seater
Visiting Supporters' Allocation: 3,000 (South
Stand)

Club Colours: Red and white striped shirts, black
shorts
Nearest Railway Station: Sunderland (one mile)
Parking (Car): Car park at ground reserved for
season ticket holders. Limited on-street parking
(but the police may decide to introduce
restrictions). Otherwise off-street parking in city
centre
Parking (Coach/Bus): As directed
Police Force and Tel No: Tyne & Wear (0191 567
6155)
Disabled Visitors' Facilities:
  Wheelchairs: 180 spots
  Blind: Commentary available
Anticipated Development(s): Work is well in
hand to extend the Stadium of Light's capacity to
47,500 and work should be completed early in
the 2000/01 season.

KEY

North direction (approx)

❶ River Wear
❷ North (Vaux) Stand (under
construction
❸ South (Metro FM) Stand
(away)
❹ To Sunderland BR station
(0.5 mile)
❺ Southwick Road
❻ Stadium Way
❼ Millennium Way
❽ Hay Street
❾ To Wearmouth Bridge (via
A1018 North Bridge Street)
to City Centre

Above: 685601; *Right:* 685695

MAY STREET

UPPER
WEST STAND
LOWER

DISABLED
PITCH SIZE
68 x105 metres
(75 x 115 yards)

AWAY FANS

METRO FM STAND

DISABLED

DISABLED

DISABLED

LOWER

VAUX STAND
UPPER

STADIUM WAY

DISABLED

McEWANS STAND

FAMILY ENCLOSURE

MILLENNIUM STAND

One of a number of clubs that now form a division between the Premier League and First Division, many fans of Sunderland — or the Black Cats (as the club's new nickname would have it) — would have welcomed simple survival. In the event, Peter Reid's team — aided by the scoring prowess of Kevin Phillips — proved to be a revelation. In the top half of the division throughout the season, indeed being second at one stage, the possibility of European football on Wearside was real. However, a mid-season dip in form and several poor results, including the home defeat by relegation-threatened Bradford City, meant that a top-half position was achieved. In 2000/01, however, with the increased capacity of the Stadium of Light cheering the team on, fans will be expecting the team to build upon this position and threaten in a more determined way for European football in 2001/02.

SWANSEA CITY

Vetch Field, Swansea SA1 3SU

Tel No: 01792 474114
Advance Tickets Tel No: 01792 462584
Fax: 01792 464120
Web Site: www.swansfc.co.uk
League: 2nd Division
Brief History: Founded 1900 as Swansea Town, changed to Swansea City in 1970. Former Grounds: various, including Recreation Ground. Moved to Vetch Field in 1912. Founder-members Third Division (1920). Record attendance 32,796
(Total) Current Capacity: 11,900 (2,500 seated)
Visiting Supporters' Allocation: 1,541 (on the West Terrace)

Club Colours: White shirts, white shorts
Nearest Railway Station: Swansea High Street
Parking (Car): Kingsway car park and adjacent Clarence Terrace (supervised car park)
Parking (Coach/Bus): As directed by Police
Police Force and Tel No: South Wales (01792 456999)
Disabled Visitors' Facilities:
  Wheelchairs: Glamorgan Street
  Blind: No special facility
Anticipated Development(s): The plans for relocation have progressed and it is now planned that the club will be playing at a new 25,000 all-seater stadium at Morfa (about two miles from Vetch Field) in August 2001.

KEY

- **C** Club Offices
- **S** Club Shop
- **E** Entrance(s) for visiting supporters
- **R** Refreshment bars for visiting supporters
- **T** Toilets for visiting supporters

↑ North direction (approx)

❶ Glamorgan Street
❷ William Street
❸ Richardson Street
❹ A4067 Oystermouth Road (8 miles to M4 Junction 42)
❺ Swansea High Street BR Station (½ mile)
❻ Supervised Car Park
❼ North Bank

Above: 615398; *Right:* 615403

After the disappointment of the failure to achieve promotion through the Play-Offs at the end of the 1998/1999 season, John Hollins' Swansea City were one of the pre-season favourites to achieve automatic promotion at the end of the 1999/2000 season and, in this, they didn't disappoint. A tussle with Rotherham United at the top of the table in the last game of the season saw the Swans achieve the championship, although the win was marred by the death of fan who was fatally injured when trampled by a police horse. However, just as there is an increasing gap between the First Division and the Premier League, so there is an increasing gap between Second and Third divisions. Swansea will need to perform well if they are to avoid the fate of local rivals, Cardiff City, and victors of the 1998/99 Play-Off final, Scunthorpe United, if they are not to make an immediate return to the Third Division.

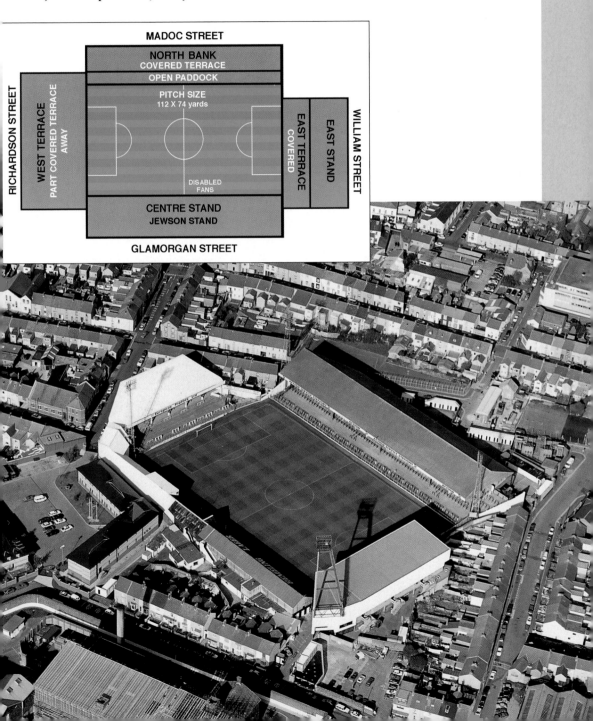

SWINDON TOWN

County Ground, County Road, Swindon, SN1 2ED

Tel No: 01793 333700
Advance Tickets Tel No: 01793 333777
Fax: 01793 333703
Web Site: http://www.swindonfc.co.uk
League: 2nd Division
Brief History: Founded 1881. Former Grounds: Quarry Ground, Globe Road, Croft Ground, County Ground (adjacent to current Ground and now Cricket Ground), moved to current County Ground in 1896. Founder-members Third Division (1920). Record attendance 32,000
(Total) Current Capacity: 15,165 (all seated)
Visiting Supporters' Allocation: 3,342 (all seated) in Arkell's Stand and Stratton Bank
Club Colours: Red shirts, white shorts
Nearest Railway Station: Swindon
Parking (Car): Town Centre
Parking (Coach/Bus): Adjacent car park

Police Force and Tel No: Wiltshire (01793 528111)
Disabled Visitors' Facilities:
  Wheelchairs: In front of Town End and Nationwide and Arkell's stands
  Blind: Commentary available
Anticipated Development(s): There are proposals – but nothing more at this time – to put a roof over the Stratton Bank End. This development, however, is opposed by local residents. Although the club is currently in administration, millionaire Terry Brady is attempting a take-over. If his plans come to fruition, he is proposing that the club relocates to a new £37 million stadium located close to the M4 and forming part of a leisure complex. There is currently no timescale for this and much will depend on how the future of the club itself unfolds.

KEY

C Club Offices
S Club Shop
E Entrance(s) for visiting supporters
R Refreshment bars for visiting supporters
T Toilets for visiting supporters

↑ North direction (approx)

❶ Shrivenham Road
❷ County Ground
❸ A345 Queens Drive (M4 Junction 15 – 3 1/2 miles)
❹ Swindon BR Station (1/2 mile)
❺ Town End
❻ Car Park
❼ County Cricket Ground
❽ Nationwide Stand
❾ Arkell's Stand

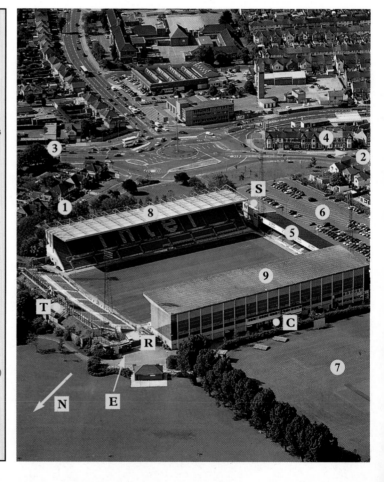

ARKELLS STAND

| AR1 | FAM | AR3 | AR4 | | AWAY |

KIDS | AR2 | **ENCLOSURE**

DISABLED FANS

PITCH SIZE
114 X 74 yards

COUNTY ROAD

TOWN END
(OVERFLOW)

STRATTON BANK STAND
(OPEN STAND)
OVERFLOW

DISABLED FANS

ENCLOSURE

| NW6 | NW5 | NW4 | NW3 | NW2 | NW1 |

SOUTH STAND

SHIVERNHAM ROAD

A disastrous season for Town both on the field and off it, saw the club's financial position deteriorate rapidly — with many of the back room staff departing and the playing staff reduced — and relegation from the First to the Second Division. Results during the season saw the dismissal of Jimmy Quinn as manager towards the end, although it is difficult to know quite how he could have improved the team's performance given the evident lack of resources. With the financial position still tenuous, any new manager will face an almighty struggle to make the club a force in the Second Division and it is hard to escape the conclusion that Swindon, like local rivals Oxford United in 1999/2000, will struggle to avoid being sucked into the relegation battle into the League's basement division.

TORQUAY UNITED

Plainmoor Ground, Torquay, TQ1 3PS

Tel No: 01803 328666
Advance Tickets Tel No: 01803 328666
Fax: 01803 323976
E-Mail: gullsfc@freeuk.com
League: 3rd Division
Brief History: Founded 1898, as Torquay
United, amalgamated with Ellacombe in 1910,
changed name to Torquay Town. Amalgamated
with Babbacombe in 1921, changed name to
Torquay United. Former Grounds:
Teignmouth Road, Torquay Recreation
Ground, Cricketfield Road & Torquay Cricket
Ground, moved to Plainmoor (Ellacombe
Ground) in 1910. Record attendance 21,908
(Total) Current Capacity: 6,003 (2,446 seated)
Visiting Supporters' Allocation: 1,004 (196
seated)
Club Colours: Yellow with white stripe shirts,
navy shorts
Nearest Railway Station: Torquay (2 miles)
Parking (Car): Street parking
Parking (Coach/Bus): Lymington Road coach
station
Police Force and Tel No: Devon & Cornwall
(01803 214491)
Disabled Visitors' Facilities:
 Wheelchairs: Ellacombe End
 Blind: Commentary available
Anticipated Development(s): There are
proposals for a joint project with a local school
for the rebuilding of the Main Stand. This
would give United a 2,500-seat stand. There
are also still plans for the redevelopment of the
Warbro End. In neither case, however, is there
a definite timescale.

KEY

C Club Offices
S Club Shop
E Entrance(s) for visiting
 supporters
R Refreshment bars for visiting
 supporters
T Toilets for visiting supporters

↑ North direction (approx)

❶ Warbro Road
❷ B3202 Marychurch Road
❸ Marnham Road
❹ Torquay BR Station (2 miles)
❺ To A38
❻ Babbacombe End

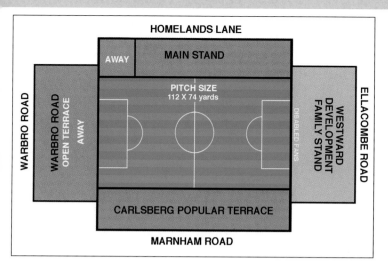

HOMELANDS LANE

MAIN STAND

AWAY

WARBRO ROAD

WARBRO ROAD OPEN TERRACE AWAY

PITCH SIZE
112 X 74 yards

DISABLED FANS

WESTWARD DEVELOPMENT FAMILY STAND

ELLACOMBE ROAD

CARLSBERG POPULAR TERRACE

MARNHAM ROAD

Although few of the Plainmoor faithful were confident, given the team's lacklustre performance in 1998/99, last season the Gulls flew high. Indeed, for much of the season a Play-Off seemed a real possibility. However, last day defeat at home to Northampton Town — which guaranteed the Cobblers automatic promotion — combined with results elsewhere (most notably Hartlepool's 3-0 win at Hull) consigned United to eighth place and, thus, another season of Third Division football for the Wes Saunders-managed team.

TOTTENHAM HOTSPUR

Bill Nicholson Way, 748 High Street, Tottenham, London N17 0AP

Tel No: 0181 365 5000
Ticket Line: 08700 112222
Fax: 0181 365 5005
Web Site: www.spurs.co.uk
League: F.A. Premier
Brief History: Founded 1882 as 'Hotspur',
changed name to Tottenham Hotspur in 1885.
Former Grounds: Tottenham Marshes and
Northumberland Park, moved to White Hart
Lane in 1899. F.A. Cup winner 1901 (as a
non-League club). Record attendance 75,038
(Total) Current Capacity: 36,257 (all seated)
Visiting Supporters' Allocation: 3,000 (in
South Stands)

Club Colours: White shirts, navy blue shorts
Nearest Railway Station: White Hart Lane
plus Seven Sisters and Manor House (tube)
Parking (Car): Street parking (min ¼ mile from
ground)
Parking (Coach/Bus): Northumberland Park
coach park
Police Force and Tel No: Metropolitan (0181
801 3443)
Disabled Visitors' Facilities:
Wheelchairs: North and South Stands (by
prior arrangement)
Blind: Commentary available
Anticipated Development(s): None planned

KEY

C Club Offices
S Club Shop
E Entrance(s) for visiting
supporters
R Refreshment bars for visiting
supporters
T Toilets for visiting supporters

↑ North direction (approx)

❶ Park Lane
❷ A1010 High Road
❸ White Hart Lane BR station
❹ Paxton Road
❺ Worcester Avenue
❻ West Stand
❼ South Stand

Although widely perceived (particularly by the White Hart Lane faithful) to be one of the 'big' teams of the Premier League, Tottenham's status has been called into doubt in recent seasons. In that respect, under George Graham, finishing in mid-table with no relegation scares might be considered an advance. The harsh reality is, however, that whilst both Arsenal and Chelsea compete for both domestic and European honours, Tottenham struggle to make any sort of impact whatsoever. With individuals such as Ginola and Anderton — when fit — in the team, Spurs certainly had a creative midfield; the team's real problem in 1999/2000 was converting this creativity into goals. Failure — with odd examples (most notably the demolition of Southampton) — to beat several of the lower teams in the division was symptomatic of Spurs' problems. During the close season, Graham will no doubt be active in the transfer market as he seeks to strengthen the squad. However, it is difficult to see the team improving sufficiently to challenge for anything other than the FA or Worthington cups, particularly with Ginola's move to Aston Villa.

TRANMERE ROVERS

Prenton Park, Prenton Road West, Birkenhead, CH42 9PY

Tel No: 0151 608 4194
Advance Tickets Tel No: 0151 609 0137
Fax: 0151 608 4385
Web Site: http://www.tranmererovers.co.uk
League: 1st Division
Brief History: Founded 1884 as Belmont F.C., changed name to Tranmere Rovers in 1885 (not connected to earlier 'Tranmere Rovers'). Former grounds: Steele's Field and Ravenshaw's Field (also known as Old Prenton Park, ground of Tranmere Rugby Club), moved to (new) Prenton Park in 1911. Founder-members 3rd Division North (1921). Record attendance 24,424

(Total) Current Capacity: 16,782 (all seated)
Visiting Supporters' Allocation: Between 2,000 and 5,842 (all seated)
Club Colours: White shirts, blue shorts
Nearest Railway Station: Hamilton Square or Rock Ferry
Parking (Car): Car park at Ground
Parking (Coach/Bus): Car park at Ground
Police Force and Tel No: Merseyside (0151 709 6010)
Disabled Visitors' Facilities:
  Wheelchairs: Main Stand
  Blind: Commentary available

KEY

C Club Offices
S Club Shop
E Entrance(s) for visiting supporters
R Refreshment bars for visiting supporters
T Toilets for visiting supporters

⬆ North direction (approx)

❶ Car Park
❷ Prenton Road West
❸ Borough Road
❹ M53 Junction 4 (B5151) – 3 miles
❺ Birkenhead (1 mile)

The past season was not without its moments of drama and controversy at Prenton Park as John Aldridge's team made limited progress up the First Division table. The team's cup form was, however, impressive, most notably in the defeat of Premier League high-fliers Sunderland 1-0 at home. The drama of the occasion was heightened by controversy when, due to confusion, Rovers substituted a player who had just been sent-off. As a result, the team finished the game with a full eleven, rather than the ten they should have had. After due deliberation, the FA allowed the result to stand (in contrast to the Worthington Cup game between West Ham and Aston Villa, when the Hammers played an ineligible player and were forced to replay the tie). Some years ago it appeared that Rovers were going to mount a sustained challenge to reach the Premier League; with the increasing gulf between the yo-yo teams at the top and the rest of the division it appears increasingly likely that the best the team can hope for is a Play-Off spot as best.

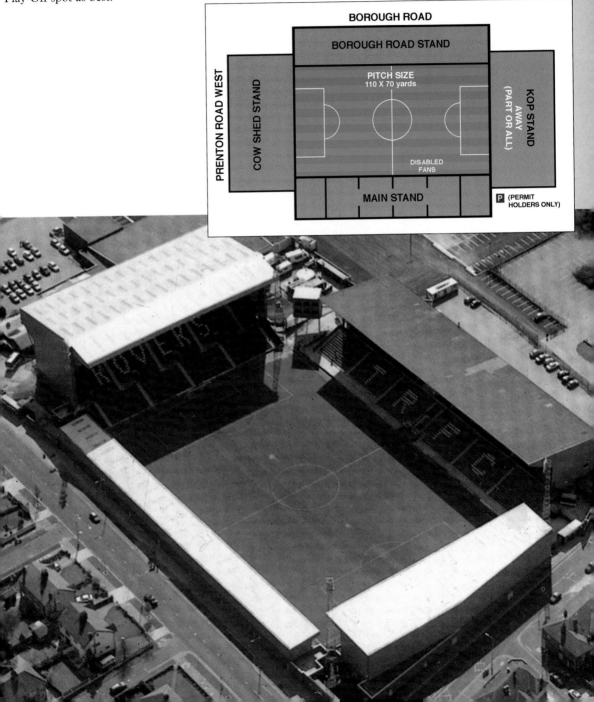

BOROUGH ROAD

BOROUGH ROAD STAND

PITCH SIZE
110 X 70 yards

PRENTON ROAD WEST

COW SHED STAND

DISABLED FANS

KOP STAND
AWAY
(PART OR ALL)

MAIN STAND

P (PERMIT HOLDERS ONLY)

WALSALL

Bescot Stadium, Bescot Crescent, Walsall, West Midlands, WS1 4SA

Tel No: 01922 622791
Advance Tickets Tel No: 01922 651410
Fax: 01922 613202
Web Site: http://www.saddlers.co.uk/
E-Mail: wfc@saddlers.co.uk
League: 2nd Division
Brief History: Founded 1888 as Walsall Town Swifts (amalgamation of Walsall Town – founded 1884 – and Walsall Swifts – founded 1885), changed name to Walsall in 1895. Former Grounds: The Chuckery, West Bromwich Road (twice), Hilary Street (later named Fellows Park, twice), moved to Bescot Stadium in 1990. Founder-members Second Division (1892). Record attendance 10,628 (25,343 at Fellows Park)
(Total) Current Capacity: 9,000 (6,700 seated)

Visiting Supporters' Allocation: 1,916 (1,916 seated)
Club Colours: Red with black shirts, black shorts
Nearest Railway Station: Bescot
Parking (Car): Car park at Ground
Parking (Coach/Bus): Car park at Ground
Police Force and Tel No: West Midlands (01922 38111)
Disabled Visitors' Facilities:
Wheelchairs: Highgate Stand
Blind: No special facility
Anticipated Development(s): Planning permission has been granted to add 3,000 to the existing Gilbert Allsop Stand. It is possible that this work will be completed in time for the start of the 1999/2000 season. This will raise the ground's capacity to 12,000.

KEY

C	Club Offices
S	Club Shop
E	Entrance(s) for visiting supporters
R	Refreshment bars for visiting supporters
T	Toilets for visiting supporters

↑ North direction (approx)

❶ Motorway M6
❷ M6 Junction 9
❸ Bescot BR Station
❹ Car Parks
❺ Bescot Crescent

Above: 685057; *Right:* 685047

P HOME
P AWAY

H.L. FELLOWS STAND

BESCOT CRESCENT

WILLIAM SHARP STAND — AWAY

PITCH SIZE
110 X 73 yards

DISABLED FANS

GILBERT ALSOP STAND — COVERED TERRACE

BANKS'S FAMILY STAND

Promoted at the end of the 1999/2000 season to the First Division under Ray Graydon, it was always going to be a struggle for Walsall to survive at the higher level. It is to the team's credit that, unlike Swindon and Port Vale, the club's ultimate fate was not finally decided until the last Sunday of the season. However, defeat at Ipswich alongside West Brom's victory over champions Charlton Athletic, condemned the Saddlers to an immediate return to the Second Division.

WATFORD

Vicarage Road Stadium, Watford, WD1 8ER

Tel No: 01923 496000
Advance Tickets Tel No: 01923 496010
Fax: 01923 496001
Web Site: www.watfordfc.com
League: 1st Division
Brief History: Founded 1898 as an
amalgamation of West Herts (founded 1891)
and Watford St. Mary's (founded early 1890s).
Former Grounds: Wiggenhall Road (Watford
St. Mary's) and West Herts Sports Ground,
moved to Vicarage Road in 1922. Founder-
members Third Division (1920). Record
attendance 34,009
(Total) Current Capacity: 22,763 (all seated)
Visiting Supporters' Allocation: 4,500 in
Vicarage Road Stand

Club Colours: Yellow shirts, red shorts
Nearest Railway Station: Watford High Street
or Watford Junction
Parking (Car): Nearby multi-storey car park in
town centre (10 mins walk)
Parking (Coach/Bus): Cardiff Road car park
Police Force and Tel No: Hertfordshire (01923
244444)
Disabled Visitors' Facilities:
Wheelchairs: Corner East Stand and South
Stand (special enclosure for approx. 24
wheelchairs), plus enclosure in North East
Corner
Blind: Commentary available in the East
Stand (20 seats, free of charge)

KEY

C Club Offices
E Club Shop

⬆ North direction (approx)

❶ Vicarage Road
❷ Occupation Road
❸ Rous Stand
❹ Town Centre (1/2 mile) – Car
Parks, High Street BR
Station
❺ Vicarage Road Stand

Two promotions in two seasons, seeing Watford move from the Second Division to the Premier League, were widely considered to foreshadow an imminent return to the Nationwide League for Graham Taylor's Watford. Although the season had its highpoints — notably the win over Liverpool — the Hornets' lack of Premier League class soon became evident and relegation back to the Nationwide League was confirmed by Easter. Fans will, however, draw encouragement from the performance of the team and, with the squad that Taylor now has in place, the team will certainly be one of the pre-season favourites for the promotion campaign in 2000/01. Welcome to the yo-yo zone!

WEST BROMWICH ALBION

The Hawthorns, Halfords Lane, West Bromwich, West Midlands, B71 4LF

Tel No: 0121 525 8888
Advance Tickets Tel No: 0121 553 5472
Fax: 0121 553 6634
Web Site: www.wba.co.uk
E-Mail: baggies@wba.co.uk
League: 1st Division
Brief History: Founded 1879. Former Grounds: Coopers Hill, Dartmouth Park, Four Acres, Stoney Lane, moved to the Hawthorns in 1900. Founder-members of Football League (1888). Record attendance 64,815
(Total) Current Capacity: 25,100 (all seated)
Visiting Supporters' Allocation: 2,100

Club Colours: Navy blue and white striped shirts, white shorts
Nearest Railway Station: Hawthorns
Parking (Car): Halfords Lane and Rainbow Stand car parks
Parking (Coach/Bus): Rainbow Stand car park
Police Force and Tel No: West Midlands (0121 554 3414
Disabled Visitors' Facilities:
  Wheelchairs: Apollo 2000 and Smethwick Road End
  Blind: Facility available

KEY

C Club Offices
S Club Shop
E Entrance(s) for visiting supporters
T Toilets for visiting supporters

↑ North direction (approx)

❶ A41 Birmingham Road
❷ M5 Junction 1
❸ Birmingham Centre (4 miles)
❹ Halfords Lane
❺ Main Stand
❻ Smethwick End
❼ Rolfe Street, Smethwick BR Station (1½ miles)
❽ The Hawthorns BR Station

With the loss of manager Denis Smith during the course of the season being symptomatic of a deeper malaise at the club, the 1999/2000 season is one that most fans of the Baggies will prefer to forget. With talented players, such as the prolific Lee Hughes, the team had the potential to reach mid-table in the First Division at the very least. In the event, West Bromwich Albion retained its First Division status only on the last day of the season when, by defeating champions Charlton Athletic at the Hawthorns combined with Walsall's defeat at Ipswich, the Saddlers were consigned to the Second Division. Unless the team's performances improve in the new season, it is difficult to see 2000/01 being anything other than another struggle against relegation, this time without — possibly — many of the talented stars.

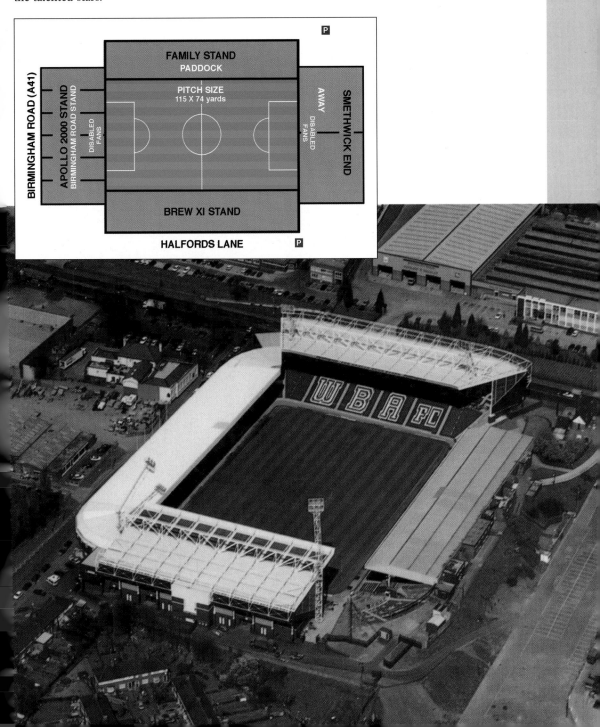

WEST HAM UNITED

Boleyn Ground, Green Street, Upton Park, London, E13 9AZ

Tel No: 020 8548 2748
Advance Tickets Tel No: 020 8548 2700
Fax: 020 8548 2758
Web Site: http://www.whufc.co.uk
League: F.A. Premiership
Brief History: Founded 1895 as Thames Ironworks, changed name to West Ham United in 1900. Former Grounds: Hermit Road, Browning Road, The Memorial Ground, moved to Boleyn Ground in 1904. Record attendance 42,322
(Total) Current Capacity: 26,052 (all seated)
Visiting Supporters' Allocation: 3,700
Club Colours: Claret and blue shirts, white shorts

Nearest Railway Station: Barking BR, Upton Park (tube)
Parking (Car): Street parking
Parking (Coach/Bus): As directed by Police
Police Force and Tel No: Metropolitan (020 8593 8232)
Disabled Visitors' Facilities:
  Wheelchairs: West Lower, Bobby Moore and Centenary Stands
  Blind: Commentaries available
Anticipated Development(s): There are tentative plans for the in-filling of the corners or of redevelopment of the West Stand but when this work will be undertaken has yet to be confirmed.

KEY

C Club Offices
S Club Shop
E Entrance(s) for visiting supporters

↑ North direction (approx)

❶ A124 Barking Road
❷ Green Stree
❸ North Stand
❹ Upton Park Tube Station (1/4 mile)
❺ Barking BR Station (1 mile)
❻ Bobby Moore Stand
❼ East Stand
❽ West Stand

One moment of folly helped to determine the Hammers' fate during the 1999/2000 season. Whilst mid-table sanctuary again beckoned Harry Redknapp's side, there was the real opportunity of bringing European football back to Upton Park through the Worthington Cup. However, semi-final victory over Aston Villa was annulled by the FA when it was discovered that the Hammers had fielded an ineligible player as substitute. Forced to replay the game, the Hammers lost and Villa found themselves as fortunate finalists. Provided that Redknapp can keep the bulk of his talented squad together — and there have been rumours of several departures during the close season — then the team ought again to threaten in both domestic cup competitions, although a sustained challenge for the Championship looks beyond the team.

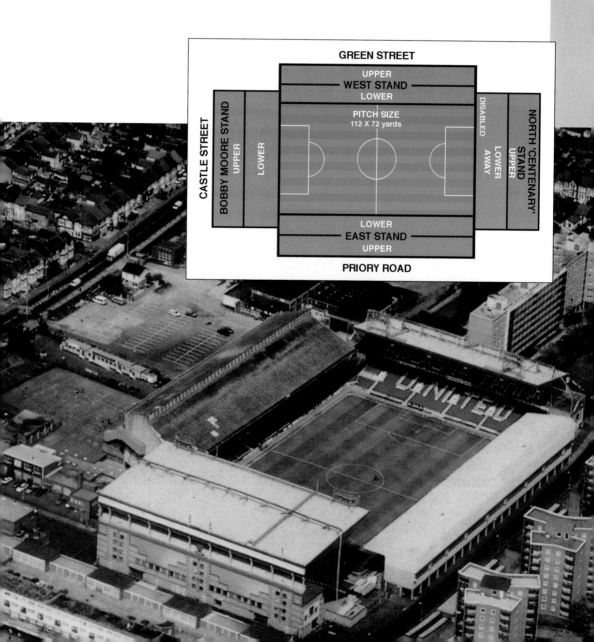

WIGAN ATHLETIC

JJB Stadium, Loire Drive, Robin Park, Wigan, Lancashire

Tel No: 01942 714000
Advance Tickets Tel No: 01942 770410
Fax: 01942 770477
League: 2nd Division
Brief History: Founded 1932. Springfield Park used by former Wigan Borough (Football League 1921-1931) but unrelated to current club. Elected to Football League in 1978 (the last club to be elected rather than promoted). Moved to JJB Stadium for start of 1999/2000 season. Record attendance at Springfield Park 27,500
(Total) Current Capacity: 25,000 (all-seated)
Visiting Supporters' Allocation: 8,178 (maximum) in East Stand (all-seated)

Club Colours: White and green shirts, white and green shorts
Nearest Railway Stations: Wigan Wallgate/Wigan North Western (both about 1.5 miles away)
Parking (Car): 2,500 spaces at the ground
Parking (Coach/Bus): As directed
Police Force and Tel No: Greater Manchester (01942 244981)
Disabled Visitors' Facilities
  Wheelchairs: 100 spaces
  Blind: No special facility although it is hoped to have a system in place shortly
Anticipated Development(s): None following completion of the ground.

KEY

C Club Offices
E Entrance(s) for visiting supporters

↑ North direction (approx)

❶ Loire Drive
❷ Anjoy Boulevard
❸ Car Parks
❹ Robin Park Arena
❺ River Douglas
❻ Leeds-Liverpool Canal
❼ To A577/A49 and Wigan town centre plus Wigan (Wallgate) and Wigan (North Western) station
❽ East Stand
❾ South Stand
❿ North Stand
⓫ West Stand

Above: 685070; Right: 685060

Football can be a cruel game. Failure in the Play-Offs at the end of the 1998/99 season cost manager Ray Mathias his job. Replacement John Benson guided Athletic to the Play-Offs again, by finishing fifth. Victory over Millwall in two hard-fought legs saw Wigan return to Wembley and a Play-Off final against Gillingham. Benson, however, decided to leave nothing to fate by announcing that he intended to stand down after the match — irrespective of the result — to move to an alternative job with the club. The Play-Off final with Gillingham was another hard fought affair, which resulted in defeat for Benson's team 3-2 after extra time. Bruce Rioch, now in the JJB Stadium hot seat, will have a team much fancied to achieve promotion but one that seems incapable of sustaining the challenge over the full season.

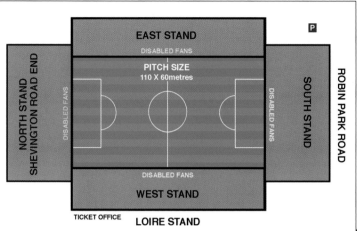

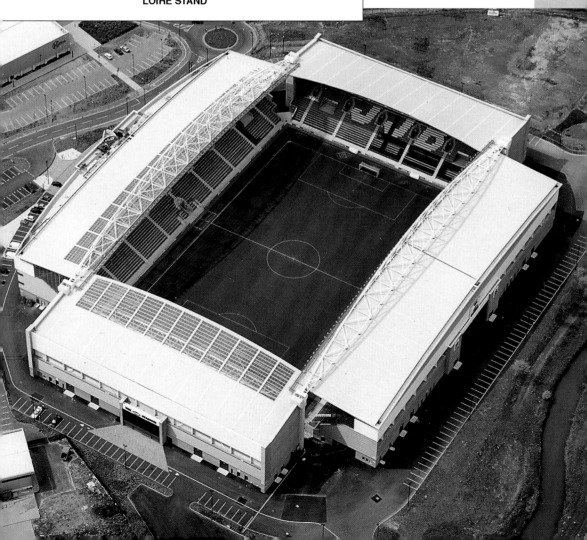

WIMBLEDON

Selhurst Park, London, SE25 6PY

Tel No: 020 8771 2233
Advance Tickets Tel No: 020 8771 8841
Fax: 020 8768 0641
Web Site: www.wimbledon-fc.co.uk
League: 1st Division
Brief History: Founded 1889 as Wimbledon Old Centrals, changed name to Wimbledon in 1905. Former Grounds: Wimbledon Common, Pepy's Road, Grand Drive, Merton Hall Road, Malden Wanderers Cricket Ground & Plough Lane. Moved to Selhurst Park (Crystal Palace F.C. Ground) in 1991. Elected to Football League in 1977. Record attendance (Plough Lane) 18,000; (Selhurst Park) 30,115
(Total) Current Capacity: 26,297 (all seated)
Visiting Supporters' Allocation: Approx 3,000
Club Colours: Blue shirts, blue shorts

Nearest Railway Station: Selhurst, Norwood Junction & Thornton Heath
Parking (Car): Street parking and Sainsbury's car park
Parking (Coach/Bus): Thornton Heath
Police Force and Tel No: Metropolitan (020 8649 1391)
Disabled Visitors' Facilities:
Wheelchairs: Park Road
Blind: Commentary available
Anticipated Development(s): Following the high profile financial problems afflicting Crystal Palace, there is a possibility that Wimbledon may acquire Selhurst Park from Ron Noades and thus cease to be tenants. However, there is nothing definite to report on this nor on the many possible sites for the club's relocation.

KEY

C Club Offices
S Club Shop
E Entrance(s) for visiting supporters
T Toilets for visiting supporters

↑ North direction (approx)

❶ Whitehorse Lane
❷ Park Road
❸ A213 Selhurst Road
❹ Selhurst BR Station (1/2 mile)
❺ Norwood Junction BR Station (1/4 mile)
❻ Thornton Heath BR Station (1/2 mile)
❼ Car Park (Sainsbury's)
❽ Holmesdale Stand

After 14 years in the top flight, the wheels finally came off the Crazy Gang's cart at the end of the season. Each season, there seems to be one team that starts off reasonably well and then ends up in free fall prior to relegation and, in 1999/2000, it was the Dons. In theory, with a successful new manager in Egil Olsen and with club under new ownership, the season should have been one of consolidation at the very least. In the event, a run of nine defeats and one draw in the final 10 games consigned to team to misery on the final Sunday of the season when, by losing at Southampton and with Bradford City defeating Liverpool, the Dons were relegated. No doubt fans will point to the harsh decisions in the six-pointer at Valley Parade as a crucial factor, but the harsh reality is that a team is rarely relegated on a single performance and, over the second half of the season, Wimbledon lacked the spirit to retain the club's Premier League position. With Olsen gone — departing after the defeat at Bradford City — and many of the star names likely to depart during the close season, Wimbledon will struggle to make an immediate return to the Premier League under new manager Terry Burton. Anyone for Second Division football in 2001/02?

WOLVERHAMPTON WANDERERS

Molineux Ground, Waterloo Road, Wolverhampton, WV1 4QR

Tel No: 01902 655000
Advance Tickets Tel No: 01902 653653
Fax: 01902 687003
Web Site: www.wolves.co.uk
E-Mail: info@wolves.co.uk
League: 1st Division
Brief History: Founded 1877 as St. Lukes, combined with Goldthorn Hill to become Wolverhampton Wanderers in 1884. Former Grounds: Old Windmill Field, John Harper's Field and Dudley Road, moved to Molineux in 1889. Founder-members Football League (1888). Record attendance 61,315
(Total) Current Capacity: 28,525 (all seated)

Visiting Supporters' Allocation: 1,500 in Jack Harris Stand or 2,971 in lower tier of John Ireland Stand
Club Colours: Gold shirts, black shorts
Nearest Railway Station: Wolverhampton
Parking (Car): West Park and adjacent North Bank
Parking (Coach/Bus): As directed by Police
Police Force and Tel No: West Midlands (01902 27851)
Disabled Visitors' Facilities:
  Wheelchairs: 164 places on two sides
  Blind: Commentary (by prior arrangement)

KEY

C Club Offices
S Club Shop
E Entrance(s) for visiting supporters
R Refreshment bars for visiting supporters
T Toilets for visiting supporters

↑ North direction (approx)

❶ Stan Cullis Stand
❷ John Ireland Stand
❸ Billy Wright Stand
❹ Ring Road – St. Peters
❺ Waterloo Road
❻ A449 Stafford Street
❼ BR Station (¹/₂ mile)
❽ Jack Harris
❾ Molineux Street
❿ Molineux Way

Despite the loss of Robbie Keane, transferred to Coventry City, and appalling early season form that saw the team in 22nd place in September, Colin Lee's Wolverhampton Wanderers fought back and, once again, just failed to miss the First Division Play-Offs. Although two wins in the last three games — against Port Vale and Fulham — ensured that Wolves were in the thick of the chase, but defeat in the third of these games, away at rivals Bolton Wanderers, meant that the Lancashire side reached the Play-Offs and consigned Wolves and the Molyneux faithful to another season of First Division football. Whether Lee remains at the club remains to see; with an apparent embargo on transfer activity and with his deputy — John Ward — being linked with management jobs elsewhere, all does not appear well at Molyneux.

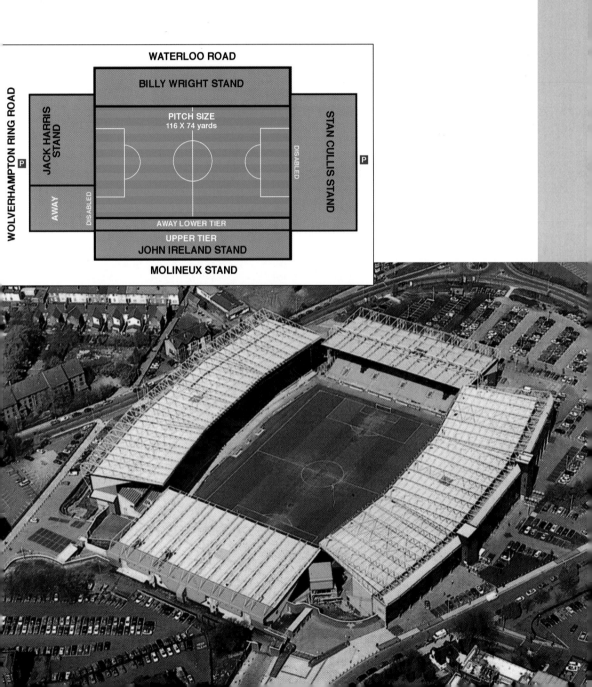

WREXHAM

Racecourse Ground, Mold Road, Wrexham, Clwyd LL11 2AN

Tel No: 01978 262129
Advance Tickets Tel No: 01978 262129
Web Site: www.wrexhamafc.co.uk
Fax: 01978 357821
League: 2nd Division
Brief History: Founded 1873 (oldest Football Club in Wales). Former Ground: Acton Park, permanent move to Racecourse Ground c.1900. Founder-members Third Division North (1921). Record attendance 34,445
(Total) Current Capacity: 15,900 (11,000 seated)
Visiting Supporters' Allocation: 3,100 (all seated)
Club Colours: Red shirts, red shorts

Nearest Railway Station: Wrexham General
Parking (Car): (Nearby) Town car parks
Parking (Coach/Bus): As directed by Police
Police Force and Tel No: Wrexham Division (01978 290222)
Disabled Visitors' Facilities:
  Wheelchairs: Mold Road Side
  Blind: No special facility
Anticipated Development(s): Following completion of the Pryce Griffiths Stand, attention will next turn to the Kop End Terrace. However, this will be retained as terracing for as long as possible and there will be no change before 2001/02 at the earliest.

KEY

C Club Offices
S Club Shop
E Entrance(s) for visiting supporters
R Refreshment bars for visiting supporters
T Toilets for visiting supporters

↑ North direction (approx)

❶ Wrexham General Station
❷ A541 – Mold Road
❸ Wrexham Town Centre
❹ Pryce Griffiths Stand
❺ Kop Town End
❻ To Wrexham Central Station

Above: 685071; *Right:* 685072

After years when the Racecourse Ground was largely a disgrace, recent improvements have seen Wrexham build a stylish new stand on the Mold Road side. On the field, there were occasional glimpses of a similar style from the team, but Brian Flynn's team finished a disappointing 11th in the Second Division. The club remains the highest placed of the trio of Welsh league teams and in 2000/01 will face a renewed challenge for local supremacy from newly-promoted Swansea City.

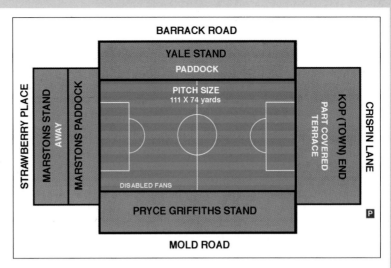

BARRACK ROAD

YALE STAND

PADDOCK

PITCH SIZE
111 X 74 yards

STRAWBERRY PLACE

MARSTONS STAND
AWAY

MARSTONS PADDOCK

DISABLED FANS

PRYCE GRIFFITHS STAND

KOP (TOWN) END
PART COVERED
TERRACE

CRISPIN LANE

P

MOLD ROAD

WYCOMBE WANDERERS

Adams Park, Hillbottom Road, Sands, High Wycombe, Bucks HP12 4HJ

Tel No: 01494 472100
Advance Tickets Tel No: 01494 441118
Fax: 01494 527633
Web Site: http://wycombewanderers.co.uk
E-Mail: wwfc@wycombewanderers.co.uk
League: 2nd Division
Brief History: Founded 1884. Former Grounds: The Rye, Spring Meadows, Loakes Park, moved to Adams Park 1990. Promoted to Football League 1993. Record attendance 15,678 (Loakes Park); 9,007 (Adams Park)
(Total) Current Capacity: 9,997 (7,306 seated)
Visiting Supporters' Allocation: 1,372
Club Colours: Sky blue with navy blue quartered shirts, blue shorts
Nearest Railway Station: High Wycombe (2$\frac{1}{2}$ miles)

Parking (Car): At Ground and Street parking
Parking (Coach/Bus): At Ground
Police Force and Tel No: Thames Valley (01296 396534)
Disabled Visitors' Facilities:
  Wheelchairs: Special shelter – Main Stand, Hillbottom Road end
  Blind: Commentary available
Anticipated Development(s): Planning permission has now been granted for the further development of the Roger Vere Stand, with the intention of adding 1,000 seats to the structure. Work will start at the end of next season and the new stand will be completed for the 2001/02 season.

KEY

C Club Offices
S Club Shop
E Entrance(s) for visiting supporters
R Refreshment bars for visiting supporters
T Toilets for visiting supporters

↑ North direction (approx)

❶ Car Park
❷ Hillbottom Road (Industrial Estate)
❸ M40 Junction 4 (approx 2 miles)
❹ Wycombe Town Centre (approx 2$\frac{1}{2}$ miles)
❺ Servispak Stand
❻ Roger Vere Stand (away)

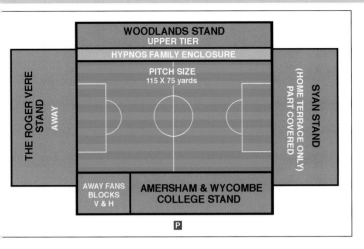

WOODLANDS STAND
UPPER TIER
HYPNOS FAMILY ENCLOSURE

PITCH SIZE
115 X 75 yards

THE ROGER VERE STAND
AWAY

SYAN STAND
(HOME TERRACE ONLY)
PART COVERED

AWAY FANS
BLOCKS
V & H

AMERSHAM & WYCOMBE
COLLEGE STAND

P

Under Lawrie Sanchez, Wanderers managed a remarkable escape from relegation at the end of the 1998/99 season when Third Division football seemed an inevitability at Adams Park — despite doing the double over Manchester City. In 1999/2000 the pundits were divided: some saw the team as odds on certainties to be relegated, others were more optimistic seeing promotion as a possibility. In the event, neither camp was correct; Wanderers achieved a position of mid-table security, finishing 12th, thus providing the team with a solid foundation for further advance in the new season.

YORK CITY

Bootham Crescent, York, YO30 7AQ

Tel No: 01904 624447
Advance Tickets Tel No: 01904 624447
Fax: 01904 631457
Web Site: www.ycfc.net
League: 3rd Division
Brief History: Founded 1922. Former ground: Fulfordgate Ground, moved to Bootham Crescent in 1932. Record attendance 28,123
(Total) Current Capacity: 8,988 (3,679 seated)
Visiting Supporters' Allocation: 2,380 (336 seated)

Club Colours: Red shirts, blue shorts
Nearest Railway Station: York
Parking (Car): Street parking
Parking (Coach/Bus): As directed by Police
Police Force and Tel No: North Yorkshire (01904 631321)
Disabled Visitors' Facilities:
Wheelchairs: In front of Family Stand
Blind: Commentary available

KEY

C Club Offices
S Club Shop
E Entrance(s) for visiting supporters
R Refreshment bars for visiting supporters
T Toilets for visiting supporters

↑ North direction (approx)

❶ Bootham Crescent
❷ Grosvenor Road
❸ Burton Stone Lane
❹ York BR Station (1 mile)

Following the trauma of the end of the 1998/99 season, when City were relegated on the last day, never having been in one of the relegation spots until the fateful last seconds of the season, most expected the team to be in a position to make a challenge for an immediate return to the Second Division. With previous manager Alan Little replaced by Neil Thompson, there were grounds for optimism, but, as so often, pre-season optimism turned to pessimism as the team wallowed in the nether regions of the Third Division. Two seasons ago, a crushing defeat at Maine Road aided Manchester City to the Play-Offs and consigned York to relegation; in 2000/01 Man City will be in Premier League and York will be facing league new boys Kidderminster Harriers — how quickly can fortunes change.

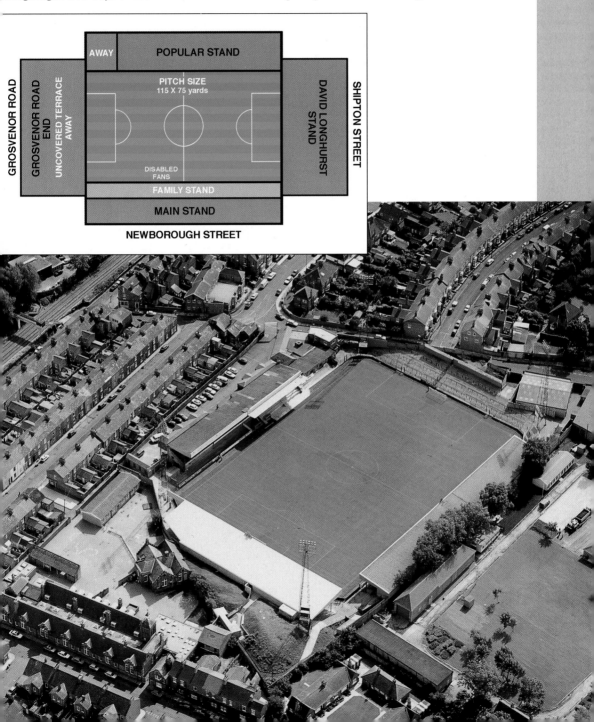

NOTES